IN WHAT BOOK ?

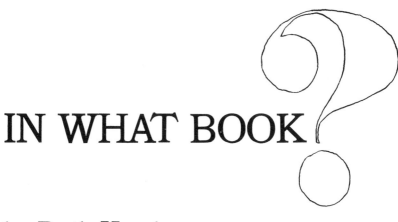

IN WHAT BOOK

by Ruth Harshaw
and Hope Harshaw Evans

Foreword by Mildred L. Batchelder

THE MACMILLAN COMPANY

COLLIER-MACMILLAN LTD., LONDON

The Macmillan Company
866 Third Avenue, New York, New York 10022

Collier-Macmillan Canada, Ltd., Toronto, Ontario

Library of Congress Catalog Card Number: 73–99122
First Printing

ACKNOWLEDGMENTS

Thanks are due to the following for permission to quote from copyrighted material:

Thomas Y. Crowell Company, Inc., for *I See the Winds* by Kazue Mizumura, Copyright © 1966 by Kazue Mizumura; and *Listen, Rabbit* by Aileen Fisher, Copyright © 1964 by Aileen Fisher.

Doubleday & Company, Inc., for *Kildee House* by Rutherford Montgomery, Copyright 1949 by Rutherford Montgomery.

Harcourt, Brace & World, Inc., for *Dancing in the Moon: Counting Rhymes* by Fritz Eichenberg; and *Sparkle and Spin* by Ann and Paul Rand.

Houghton Mifflin Company for *My Friend Mac* by May McNeer and Lynd Ward.

Little, Brown and Company for *Dead End School* by Robert Coles; and *The Wing on a Flea* by Ed Emberley.

Lothrop, Lee & Shepard Company, Inc., for *A For the Ark* by Roger Duvoisin, Copyright © 1948 by Lothrop, Lee & Shepard Company, Inc.; and *Little Bear's Sunday Breakfast* by Janice and Mariana, Copyright © 1958 by Lothrop, Lee & Shepard Company, Inc.

McGraw-Hill Book Company for *Whiskers, My Cat* by Letta Schatz.

Random House, Inc., for *Horton Hatches the Egg* by Dr. Seuss, Copyright 1940 and renewed 1968 by Dr. Seuss.

Foreword

What a history of sharing the delights of good books was Ruth Harshaw's life! With her family—first her children and the neighbors', and then with grandchildren one after another as they came along. With the children in her school classes for whom she wrote two books of mythology. With children throughout the Chicago area whose families discovered in the mid-thirties the Carson Pirie Scott and Company Hobby Horse Book Club Foundation Library Plan. (This plan, made by Ruth Harshaw as the educational consultant at the store, provided that good books, books of permanent value, be sent to boys and girls on a bimonthly or a monthly basis. The 1936 list was so well chosen that a 1969 child who read the books included would have a rewarding reading experience and, too, would gain the background to understand many often-used allusions to literature.) Sharing also with the children who took part in and listened to the two radio programs, "Battle of Books" and "Carnival of Books," each week for more than twenty years. And it was not only the children who found pleasure in reading the books she introduced so vividly. It was parents and teachers at innumerable P.T.A. meetings. It was also librarians who discovered new enthusiasms through her introductions and who admired and, within their abilities, emulated her methods.

Yes, Ruth Harshaw was a genius at sharing good books with others.

What made her so? Many things, of course, but among them her interest in individual people, children and adults, readers and authors. She read the flood of children's books—and many other books, also—with sympathy and understanding and, at the same time, with critical appreciation of the style and quality which make for endurance.

More children with the chance and desire to read books worth reading, more parents who know the importance of sharing reading with their children, more libraries with generous collections of good books and with librarians who share reading pleasure, more teachers who keep up to date with the best of children's books and share what they find—these were the goals Ruth Harshaw worked for, and in doing so enlisted the help of any and all who were interested or could be interested in forwarding these objectives.

Think of all the thousands of people of all ages who, through Ruth Harshaw, found a book that was important to them. In most cases they might not remember how that book first came to their attention. Little matter. The book became a continuing experience for enjoying and reenjoying, for passing on to others.

Among those most appreciative of Ruth Harshaw's enthusiastic and ingenious way of stirring interest in books were librarians and teachers. They seized on her book, done with Dilla MacBean, called *What Book Is*

That?, published in 1948 by Macmillan. Here were samples of questions which had been used on the Chicago Board of Education program, "Battle of Books." These were used and reused in libraries and classrooms all across the country. Librarians had long encouraged Mrs. Harshaw to give them a much more generous compilation of book questions, for her questions were more intriguing than those of many who tried this technique. And thus the new book was started. With her daughter Hope Harshaw Evans, she worked on it for a year before her death in 1968. Mrs. Evans, who had assisted her mother for many years in the extensive reading and preparation of the two radio programs, completed the book they had planned and worked on together. *In What Book?* is the very satisfactory result. It will help many librarians and teachers and parents to introduce books in interesting ways and, equally important, to know about books worth introducing. It is one more extension of Ruth Harshaw's book sharing, and all who use the book will gain in their pleasure in enjoying books with children.

Mildred L. Batchelder

Evanston, Illinois

Preface

I know of no greater single pleasure our family has had than that of reading aloud—sharing the fun, the adventure, the sorrow or the struggle in such stories as *Winnie-the-Pooh, The Long Winter, Little Britches* or *Children of Green Knowe.* The people in these books became a part of our family. "Don't be an Eeyore," we might say to someone feeling sorry for himself. And there were many years when Ralph Moody, or Little Britches, was the seventh member of our family. "Measure twice and saw once," as Ralph's father told him, is a household saying in our home.

Having Ruth Harshaw as a grandmother heightened our children's appreciation of good reading. "Certainly, if you go to the grocery store once a week, you take your children to the library once a week," she said again and again to friends, to family and to the thousands of parents and teachers before whom she often spoke. Having followed this belief herself as a parent, when her own children were grown she reached out to urge other children and other families to share the pleasure of reading.

For many years she and Dilla MacBean, director of

school libraries in Chicago, cooperated to present "Battle of Books," an in-school broadcast of a book quiz program, whose contestants were teams of students from two different Chicago public schools each week. This program was on the air over twenty-five years in Chicago, produced by the Division of Libraries of the Chicago Public Schools. Offering sample questions from this program, a book was published by The Macmillan Company in 1948 called *What Book Is That?* Included in *What Book Is That?* were dramatic sketches from books. These short sketches, usually a brief conversation between two characters, were another way of presenting a book for the teams to identify. But the questions about books comprised the major part of the radio program "Battle of Books." Over the years Chicago school children sent in thousands and thousands of questions about books they enjoyed. These questions were edited by Ruth Harshaw and used on the program.

Two years ago the Macmillan Children's Book Department asked Ruth Harshaw to do a book of questions based on outstanding books for children—books which have been favorites for years, and newer books which have helped children develop a love for good reading. This new book was to include questions from several hundred books. The job would be a long and exciting one, and it was with pleasure that I accepted the opportunity to help in this undertaking. Months of enjoyable reading followed in order to write the questions for *In What Book?* We began this work in 1967, and it was completed after Ruth Harshaw's death.

Following are the lists from which we chose recommended books to be included:

American Library Association:
Let's Read Together, 1960 and 1964.
Notable Children's Books, 1940–1959 and subsequent years.
Books for Children, 1960–1965, 1965–1966, 1966–1967 and 1967–1968.
Best Books of 1966, 1967 and 1968 from *School Library Journal*.

Children's Booklist for Small Public Libraries published by the University of the State of New York, 1958 and 1964.

Children's Books compiled by Virginia Haviland and Lois B. Watt for the Library of Congress, 1964–1968.

"Children's Classics" by Alice M. Jordan (*The Horn Book Magazine*, 1947).

"Fanfare," *The Horn Book*'s Honor List of Children's Books, 1958–1968.

Good Books for Children, Bulletin of the Center for Children's Books, edited by Mary K. Eakin, 1948–1961 and 1950–1965 (University of Chicago Press).

Newbery and Caldecott medal winners and runner-ups.

We Build Together, National Council of Teachers of English, edited by Charlemae Rollins, 1967.

H. W. Wilson Company:
The Children's Catalog, Eleventh Edition 1966, and 1967, 1968 supplements.
Junior High School Library Catalog, First Edition 1965 and later supplements.

In What Book? contains over four hundred questions which are organized into four general categories. We found it very difficult to assign a book to a specific age level because different children enjoy books at a different age. And there are many books enjoyed by everyone

from seven to seventy. So you will find deliberate over-
lap from one section to another. For instance, there is a
question from A. A. Milne in the first section, "For the
Very Young," and another one in the third section, "For
Readers in the Middle Years." Henry Huggins is introduced in the second section, "For Young Readers," and
again in the third section. And the Laura Ingalls Wilder
books are represented in three sections. Therefore, we
intend these divisions to be flexible guidelines for use
and enjoyment of the questions.

I. For the Very Young (ages 3–6)
Here are questions from nursery rhyme and picture books
such as: *The Box with Red Wheels* by the Petershams,
Curious George by H. A. Rey, *Play with Me* by Marie Hall
Ets and *Make Way for Ducklings* by Robert McCloskey.

II. For Young Readers (ages 4–8)
More picture books are in this section, though with longer
stories, also fables, fairy tales and books such as: *Father
Bear Comes Home* by Else Holmelund Minarik, *Project Cat*
by Nellie Burchardt, *Home Is the Sailor* by Rumer Godden
and *Ellen Tebbits* by Beverly Cleary.

III. For Readers in the Middle Years (ages 8–12)
This is the largest category, intended for the hungry readers
in the upper elementary grades. Some of the titles are:
Little Vic by Doris Gates, *More All-Of-A-Kind Family* by
Sydney Taylor, *Peter Pan* by James M. Barrie, *The Borrowers*
by Mary Norton and *Henry Reed's Journey* by Keith Robertson.

IV. For Older Readers (ages 12 up)
The questions in this section come from books for the upper
grades and early teens, such as: *Calico Bush* by Rachel
Field, *Durango Street* by Frank Bonham, *Wilderness Bride*
by Annabel and Edgar Johnson, *The Little Fishes* by Erik
Christian Haugaard and *Lions in the Way* by Bella Rodman.

Every book about which a question has been written has been chosen and read with care. Because of limited space we have not been able, as often as we would like, to mention more than one title by one author. We have done this occasionally when we felt an author's books appealed to readers of different ages or of varied interests, and in a few instances to demonstrate a different type of question. There are many worthy titles which might have been included. And perhaps the children you know will write questions about them. But if the children in your home, your school, your library, know the answers to the questions in this book, you will know that they are reading some of the best books published for young people.

Hope Harshaw Evans

Stamford, Connecticut

Contents

Have Fun with
In What Book?

An Introduction by Ruth Harshaw

Because I think having fun with children is fundamental to establishing warm, personal, lasting friendship and understanding, I planned for fun, whether as a parent, a teacher, a grandmother or a radio moderator. And because I believe that one of the greatest things we have to give a child during his preschool and school years is a love of reading, I spent much time planning how to do this. A lecture now and then about good books will never do. We must have fun with books! And because Dilla MacBean, formerly director of the Division of Libraries of the Chicago Public Schools, and Dr. Miriam E. Peterson, the present director, felt as I did, "Battle of Books" was launched on the air where it has stayed over twenty-five years. From this belief of mine, that it is important to love reading, came also the radio program "Carnival of Books," the book *What Book Is That?* and now *In What Book?* It has been fun!

Even after twenty-five years of practice, it is still a challenge to write a good question about a book. I find it takes more thought to write a good question than it does to write a book review. A question must be interesting, specific and stimulating. It should be so interesting that you enjoy hearing the question, even if you do not know the answer. It should be so specific that if you have read the book you will know the answer. It should be so stimulating that if you have *not* read the book, you will want to. It is not concerned with minute details or names of unimportant characters or places. It is about the main event, the main person or the main theme of the book. When it is possible, additional clues to the answer are helpful and add to the enjoyment. I find that I must have the book in my hand to write a good question, and that I must think very carefully, or my question does not refer only to the book before me.

For instance, I might write:

> "Can you put these characters in the right book: Willie and Georgie?"

Now Willie and Georgie are not unusual names, even though the book I have in mind is a very famous one, *Rabbit Hill* by Robert Lawson. There might be a Willie and a Georgie in several books. So I might write the question this way:

> "Of what book do these clues remind you: Willie, Georgie, a rain barrel, an eighteen-foot brook?"

This is more specific now, and more interesting. Or I might ask the question about *Rabbit Hill*, describing specific action:

> "In what book does a rabbit make local history by leaping over an eighteen-foot brook to escape from a dog?"

Beginning with the questions in this book a parent, teacher or librarian can work out quiz games to develop interest in reading. If you do this at home, various members of the family may want to be quizmaster. If you are working with a class or large group and choose teams, using only six or eight boys and girls, everyone else in the room can score himself on the answers. You may want to appoint two people to act as secretaries to write down titles used, and from this develop a reading list.

On the radio program we gave ten points for a correct answer, and less if we added a clue. But the scoring is not as important as keeping the spirit of fun.

However you plan your quiz game, you will soon find the children wanting to write questions about books they are reading. They will think at first that this is very easy. Only after writing some questions and reading them over will they learn how to think clearly about a book, to be able to pick out the main theme or distinguishing traits in leading characters, in order to write a question which applies just to that book. Or they may become aware of similar characters or events in several books and write comparative questions, such as:

> "What is similar in these two books, in addition to the word courage in each title: *Li Lun, Lad of Courage* by Carolyn Treffinger and *Call It Courage* by Armstrong Sperry?
>
> Answer: In both books the leading character is accused of being a coward and struggles fiercely to disprove the accusation."

When the boys and girls in your family, your classroom or your library are writing interesting, stimulating, specific questions, then you will know they are understanding and appreciating the books they read.

Some schools I know have formed book clubs, and admission to the weekly meeting is a question about a book. These questions are read aloud, discussed and perhaps improved with the help of the club. In other schools, one classroom will challenge another to a book quiz contest. The boys in some families challenge the girls, and in others the parents team up against the children. You may think of other ways to stimulate reading with these questions. Use *In What Book?* and have fun!

~ I ~

For the Very Young

Questions *

1. If you were the character in this nursery rhyme, what would you do "To see an old lady upon a white horse"?

2. In *The Box with Red Wheels* by the Petershams, what is the strange thing that all of the curious animals see when they peer into the box?

3. Was it a giant, a witch or a troll who tried to stop the billy goats from going over a bridge in "The Three Billy Goats Gruff"?

4. Who is the little boy who went for a walk with a crayon and drew himself some wonderful adventures?

5. In *The Bundle Book* by Ruth Krauss, a mother sees a strange bundle under the blankets in her bed. What is it?

6. Where would you read about a garbage man called Stan, and a garbage truck called Emily which was *empty* when it had finished its day's work collecting garbage?

7. In *The Storm Book* by Charlotte Zolotow, a little boy watches a summer storm come. He sees the lightning, hears the thunder, watches the rain. What is the last thing he sees, after the storm has ended?

8. If you know the counting book called *Brown Cow Farm* by Dahlov Ipcar, then you probably know how many brown cows there were and how many brown calves.

9. What very shy and bashful boy went out one Sun-

day to find his Granny's earring which she had lost on the way home from church?

10. In what book do the rabbits finish painting the eggs for Easter when, crickle crackle, all the eggs pop open?

11. Cat lovers will probably know the name of the cat that is described by this rhyme:
    "During the night he's a fire-eyed prowler.
    A bristle-haired hisser.
    A fighter.
    A growler."

12. What's the name of the nursery rhyme character who was found under the haystack fast asleep?

13. What book tells how the sun, with gentle warmth, was able to outdo the strength and fury of the North Wind?

14. In what book does a poor boy set out to entertain the king? He is helped by an old woman, a whistle made from an enchanted twig and an army of rabbits.

15. In the book *Just Me* by Marie Hall Ets, a little boy tries to walk like his cat and his rooster. He tries to hop like a rabbit, wriggle like a snake and imitate other animals. What does he do when he sees his father at the pond getting into his boat?

16. In the book *Mike's House* by Julia L. Sauer, why did Robert call the public library "Mike's House"?

17. In the book *The Mitten* by Alvin Tresselt, what happens to the mitten dropped in the snow by the little boy who has been gathering wood for his grandmother?

18. Who is the small boy who begins to cry because his mother sends him out of the kitchen, his brother tells him not to touch his schoolbooks, his sister yells at him for touching her paper dolls and, finally, his father scolds him for touching his typewriter?

19. If one night you left the leather cut to make a pair of shoes, and in the morning you found the shoes all made and ready to sell, who would you be?

20. In what book does a teddy bear in a department store go searching for a button to replace the one that's missing on his overalls strap?

21. Can you name these two picture books about snow?
   a) One tells of birds and animals preparing for winter, but a very hard winter comes, and so a little old man and a little old woman help the creatures by spreading food on the snow.
   b) The other book tells about a boy named Peter playing in the snow. Both of these books won a Caldecott Medal.

22. In what book would you find these counting rhymes?
   "2 moose scaring a papoose"
   "10 cats trying on hats"
   "14 mice skating on ice."

23. What's the name of the tale in which an old woman gave a cow some hay, so she could have some milk to feed a cat, so the cat would start to kill a rat, so the old woman could get home that night?

24. Who would you be, and in what book, if you got out of bed at night to tell your parents there's a tiger in your room, then again because you think

there is a giant, and still again because the curtains are moving?

25. What lion finds the door to his house in the zoo open, and so he takes a walk through town? He is surprised because everyone who sees him faints or screams or runs away.

26. In what book do a boy and his grandfather go in search of a red, white and blue butterfly? While looking for it, they fall into a hole in the ground which leads them into an old cave with paintings on the wall.

27. Here is a conversation. Do you remember the book? A man and an animal are talking.
    " 'Where is your wife, Mr. Leopard?'
    " 'She will come with the P's, Mr. Noah. She thinks our other name, PANTHER, sounds better.' "

28. In the book *May I Bring a Friend?* by Beatrice Schenk de Regniers, a little boy is invited often to eat with the king and queen, and each time he goes he asks if he may bring a friend. Can you name some of the friends he brings?

29. In what book would you find this rhyme?
    "Words are the names of people you like:
    Sally and Mary,
    Thomas and Harry.
    Words tell how you feel:
    Fine and dandy
    And I like candy."

30. In the book *One Monday Morning* by Uri Shulevitz, a king and a queen and a little prince come every day to see a little boy, but he isn't home. One day he is on a subway, another day he is at the laundromat, and another day he's shopping for groceries.

Each day more royal visitors come with the king. At last, on Sunday, the little boy *is* home when the visitors bring what with them?

31. A house of straw, a house of sticks,/an ugly wolf, a house of bricks. What story does this rhyme describe?

32. In order to prove which one was the prettiest, who bit and scratched and clawed one another until all were eaten up?

33. Why would a little girl have her mother trade Daddy's feather bed, and Daddy could sleep in horsey's bed, and horsey could sleep in sister's bed?

34. What little animal tells his mother that he is going to run away and become a sailboat, but his mother says that then she will be the wind and blow him where she wants him?

35. Can you name these two books by Marjorie Flack?
    a) In one, a curious little dog is chased by two white ducks.
    b) In another, a little boy gets advice from a bear.

36. Who went to the cupboard to give her poor dog a bone and found the cupboard bare?

37. If you saw koala bears all dressed in costumes, dancing and having a wonderful time, what book would you be reading?

38. In what picture book would you find this rhyme?
    "A triangle is
    A finny fish-tail
    An ice-cream cone,
    A harpoon for a whale."

39. What little kitten has a sad time because he tries to

be a rooster, a goat, a duck and a rabbit, until he decides he wants to be a kitten?

40. Four children at night run barefoot in the grass, sit in a tree and run and hide from a giant shadow moving across the lawn, in what book?

41. What stuffed bear was put in a washing machine by mistake, then in a dryer? When he came out he was so clean and fluffy that the little girl who owned him didn't recognize him.

42. Who wound his clock, setting the alarm for April, before going to bed, and when he woke up began his morning exercises this way?
    "One-two I hate the zoo.
    Three-four I go to the store.
    Five-six I hunt for ticks."

43. For her birthday, a little girl wants to go outside at night with her father, to see what bees and moths, flowers and dandelions, frogs, rabbits and other creatures do at night. Can you name this book?

44. In what two folk tales does a little girl walk into a house without knocking?

45. Do you know the name of the kitten that a little boy bought for a quarter? When it was lost, the boy wanted his father to give the man who found it a thousand dollars as reward.

46. In the story *Davy and His Dog* by Lois Lenski, where does Davy's dog hide when Davy is ready to give him a bath?

47. Who is the mouse who stored words instead of food when the animals were getting ready for winter?

Later, during the winter when the mice were cold and hungry, he told them of the warm sun and the beauty of the seasons.

48. Where did the Rat wear a feather in his hat, and where did the Lion have a green and yellow tie on?

49. In what book does a little girl long for a fancy flowered hat, and is disappointed when her aunt sends a plain white hat? She wears the hat to church, but on the way home strange things begin to happen and soon her hat is not plain!

50. Can you put the name of a season in these two titles?
    a) *The ___ Snowman.*
    b) *___ time for Jeanne-Marie.*

51. What unhappy creature was unwanted by his family because he did not look like his brothers and sisters? After awhile he learns that this is not his real family, and as he grows he becomes truly a beautiful bird.

52. What happens when a friendly man, on a stormy night, invites into his little house every traveler who passes by, in the book called *Always Room for One More* by Sorche Nic Leodhas?

53. Can you name another little creature, like Rumpelstiltskin, who helped a girl spin five skeins a day for a king, but warned her that at the end of a month he would take her away unless she could guess his name?

54. Chester sat under a tree so deep in his thoughts he never saw the lady in the automobile collide with the armored car right in front of him, though all

about people were reaching for the fifty-dollar bills that blew out of the armored car. What book is this?

55. In *Winnie-the-Pooh* by A. A. Milne, who received for his birthday an empty jar which had had honey in it and the remains of a broken balloon?

56. Who is the lonely striped cat in Venice who wants very much to have a home? He is often hungry, and one night, fighting for food with a big black cat, he falls into a canal.

57. The Dog gathered many large shells and stones, strung them on a liana fiber and wore it on his neck. The loud noise made all the jungle animals think he was a monster. What book is it?

58. In what book does a fortuneteller help a sheep find her mistress by telling the sheep to go to the fair and look there?

59. Because a rooster listens to a fox praise his singing, he is caught by the fox. Then, when the fox follows the clever rooster's advice, he loses his captive. What is the name of this old tale?

60. In the picture book *The Egg Tree* by Katherine Milhous, Katy and Carl and the cousins go on an Easter egg hunt at Grandmother's farm. What does Katy find instead of the eggs that had been hidden for the hunt?

61. In *The Story of Babar, the Little Elephant* by Jean de Brunhoff, when Babar runs away from the hunter and goes to the city, an old lady gives him her purse. What are the first things he buys?

62. In what book does a kitten argue with an island?

The kitten tells the island that because water is all around it the island is not part of the world.

63. A little girl goes blueberry picking with her mother, but so does a bear cub and *his* mother—and there is an exciting mix-up. What book is this?

64. What book tells the story of the red cock who crowed in the middle of the night to save his master's life? After five nights of this the neighbors said the farmer would have to get rid of the cock if he woke them all again.

65. In this story a mouse becomes a friend to a dove in a cage because the dove is sad and lonely for the out of doors and lets the mouse have his food. What book is this?

66. What book tells you to say, "Excuse me," if you walk backward and bump into a crocodile, and tells you to say, "How do you do?" when you are introduced to an elephant?

67. If you can name the pet snake who captured a robber, you will name this book.

68. What mouse became a business mouse by going secretly at night into a cheese factory, tasting the cheese and then pinning notes on each cheese, giving advice on the flavor?

69. In an old song and in a picture book of the same name, a fox goes hunting and takes home a gray goose and a duck. Do you know the name of the book?

70. In what story would you read of this chain of events? A bird plans to pounce on a squirrel's head,

because the squirrel is going to bite a monkey's tail, when the monkey drops a coconut on a tiger who is waiting to pounce on a camel.

71. Who owned a steam shovel named Mary Anne that dug, in one day, a cellar for the new town hall in Popperville?

72. Despite all kinds of weather and dangers, in what book does an elephant stay on the job, and say again and again:
    "I meant what I said
    And I said what I meant. . . .
    An elephant's faithful
    One hundred per cent!"

73. What monkey upset a museum when he knocked over a palm tree which fell on a dinosaur, knocking the dinosaur down, too?
    Clue: The director of the museum is very angry until he learns that this monkey will help with one of his experiments.

74. Who would you be if you were in a hospital and eleven little girls and a lady came to see you at one time?

75. In what book does a little boy named Juan prepare a garden in front of his house in the hope that swallows will come there to nest?

76. Do you know the book about the wind which says:
    "May wind is busy
    Brushing the robin's tail,
    Combing the willow tree,
    And whispering to my ear
    That summer is near."

77. What is similar in these two books, and what is the big difference?

a) *Anatole and the Cat* by Eve Titus.
b) *Belling the Tiger* by Mary Stolz.

78. In what book does a small boy fall in a well, and because his name is so long he almost is not rescued?

79. A boy named Max put on his wolf suit one night and told his mother he would eat her up. She sent him to his room, and then what happened? He went on a trip to __ __ __ __ __ (also the name of the book).

80. A little boy named Jay brings home a very small pet which he keeps in a little cage on his bedside table. At night it sings. On Jay's first day of school he takes his pet in his pocket, and because it is dark in there it sings in school. Do you know this book?

81. In what book does a fox hide under a barn on a ranch to escape from a fire? When he comes out he is hungry, but the little animals he usually hunts have all run away.

82. Have you ever been in a traffic jam? In what three books was traffic stopped because:
    a) a monkey landed on top of a traffic light?
    b) a mother duck wanted to take her eight children across a busy Boston street?
    c) a pigeon tried to dry his feathers in a green "GO" light?

83. In what book does a little boy say to an animal:
    ". . . do you know what I'd do
    if I had antennae ears
    like you?
    I'd hop, hop, hop to a candy shop
    and listen to every last lollipop!"

84. What little bird had the most beautiful wings in the world, but his friends didn't like him because he looked different? So gradually he gave away his golden feathers and plain black ones took their place.

85. In what book does a fried cake lead a boy on a wild chase down a mountain and up again, back to the poor little farm he'd started from, but now the boy isn't the only one chasing the fried cake?

86. What dog was so huge that when his owner took him to Africa he had to travel on a barge pulled by a tugboat?

87. In what book does a young bear play one summer with a girl named Emily who has a doll named Lucy? When summer ends and Emily must go back to school, she gives the bear a gift and he gives her one.

88. What book tells the story of a proud turtle named Solon who accuses a king of talking too much? One day, while Solon is hanging onto a stick which is held at each end by a flying bird, he wants the birds to fly lower so he can be seen better.

89. What hen took a walk with a fox sneaking along behind her and led that fox into a sack of flour and a stream of bees?

90. Who are the two children in the tale in which a witch says:
    "Nibble, nibble like a mouse,
    Who is nibbling at my house?"

91. What little horse, who wanted more than anything to jump the brook the way his mother did, fell

asleep one day and dreamed that he had a pair of silvery wings?

92. In the well-known nursery rhyme in which a cat had a fiddle, what did the cow do?

93. In the story *The Little Engine That Could* by Watty Piper, what was in the train that was stuck on the mountain?

94. A friendly little troll walks around a lonely farm at night and talks to the animals. What is his name?

95. What little girl was good as gold until she lost her first tooth? Then things began to go wrong. She lost things. She forgot things. And one day, while shopping in a big store, she lost her mother! Her name is the name of this book.

Answers

1. I would "Ride a cock horse to Banbury Cross," as found in the *Book of Nursery and Mother Goose Rhymes* compiled and illustrated by Marguerite de Angeli.

2. They see a baby in the box.

3. It was a troll in the old tale by Peter C. Asbjörnsen and Jörgen I. Moe, retold for the very young in Marcia Brown's *The Three Billy Goats Gruff.*

4. Harold in *Harold and the Purple Crayon* by Crockett Johnson.

5. It is the mother's little girl.

6. In the book *Dear Garbage Man* by Gene Zion.

7. He sees a beautiful rainbow.

8. Ten brown cows and ten brown calves.

9. Benjie, in the book of that name by Joan M. Lexau.

10. *Happy Easter* by Kurt Wiese.

11. Whiskers, in the book *Whiskers, My Cat* by Letta Schatz.

12. Little Boy Blue, found in *The Real Mother Goose* illustrated by Blanche Fisher Wright.

13. *The North Wind and the Sun* by Jean de la Fontaine, illustrated by Brian Wildsmith.

14. *Two Hundred Rabbits* by Lonzo Anderson.

15. He runs, "like nobody else at all, just me."

16. Because Robert's favorite book was *Mike Mulligan*

and His Steam Shovel and the library was where he found the book, so he called it Mike's House.

17. Many different animals crawl into the mitten to get out of the cold.

18. Sam, in the book called *Sam* by Ann Herbert Scott.

19. The shoemaker, in "The Shoemaker and the Elves" by the Brothers Grimm, retold and illustrated for the very young in Adrienne Adams' book of that name.

20. *Corduroy* by Don Freeman.

21. a) *The Big Snow* by Berta and Elmer Hader.
    b) *The Snowy Day* by Ezra Jack Keats.

22. *Dancing in the Moon: Counting Rhymes* by Fritz Eichenberg.

23. "The Old Woman and Her Pig," from *English Fairy Tales* by Joseph Jacobs, retold and illustrated for the very young in Paul Galdone's *The Old Woman and Her Pig.*

24. Frances, a badger, in *Bedtime for Frances* by Russell Hoban.

25. The Happy Lion, in the book of that name by Louise Fatio.

26. *The Butterfly Chase* by Denise and Alain Trez.

27. *A for the Ark* by Roger Duvoisin.

28. He brings a giraffe, a hippopotamus, monkeys, an elephant, lions and a seal.

29. *Sparkle and Spin* by Ann and Paul Rand.

30. On Sunday they bring a little dog.

31. "The Story of the Three Little Pigs," from *English Fairy Tales* by Joseph Jacobs, retold and illustrated for the very young in L. Leslie Brooke's *The Golden Goose Book.*

32. Millions of Cats, in the book of that name by Wanda Gág.

33. Because the little girl wanted her mother to get the money to buy her a china doll, in the book *Mommy, Buy Me a China Doll* by Harvé and Margot Zemach.

34. The bunny, in *The Runaway Bunny* by Margaret Wise Brown.

35. a) *Angus and the Ducks.*
    b) *Ask Mr. Bear!*

36. Old Mother Hubbard, found in *Mother Goose: Seventy-Seven Verses* with pictures by Tasha Tudor.

37. *Bear Party* by William Pène du Bois.

38. *The Wing on a Flea* by Ed Emberley. The book begins:
    "A triangle is
    The wing on a flea
    And the beak on a bird,
    If you'll just look and see."

39. Pitschi, in the book of that name by Hans Fischer.

40. *The Moon Jumpers* by Janice May Udry.

41. Theodore, in the book of that name by Edward Ormondroyd.

42. Little Bear, in *Little Bear's Sunday Breakfast* by Janice and Mariana.

43. *In the Middle of the Night* by Aileen Fisher.

44. Goldilocks in "The Story of the Three Bears," and Snow White in "Snow White and the Seven Dwarfs," from *Illustrated Treasury of Children's Literature* edited by Margaret E. Martignoni.

45. Mittens, in the book *Mittens* by Clare Turlay Newberry.

46. In the bureau drawer.

47. Frederick, in the book of that name by Leo Lionni.

48. Johnny Crow's garden, in the book of that name by L. Leslie Brooke.

49. *Jennie's Hat* by Ezra Jack Keats.

50. a) *The Summer Snowman* by Gene Zion.
    b) *Springtime for Jeanne-Marie* by Françoise.

51. The Ugly Duckling, in the story of that name by Hans Christian Andersen.

52. The house collapses. Then all the visitors help build a bigger house.

53. Tom Tit Tot, in the book of that name retold and illustrated by Evaline Ness.

54. *Nothing Ever Happens on My Block* by Ellen Raskin.

55. Eeyore the donkey.

56. Felice, in the book of that name by Marcia Brown.

57. *The Coconut Thieves* by Catharine Fournier.

58. *Jeanne-Marie at the Fair* by Françoise.

59. *Chanticleer and the Fox,* retold and illustrated by Barbara Cooney.

60. Packed away in the attic, she finds six hollow eggs

painted with beautiful pictures—eggs to be hung on an egg tree.

61. A green suit, a shirt, a tie and a derby hat.

62. *The Little Island* by Golden MacDonald and Leonard Weisgard.

63. *Blueberries for Sal* by Robert McCloskey.

64. *The Cock and the Ghost Cat* by Betty Jean Lifton.

65. *The Mousewife* by Rumer Godden.

66. *What Do You Say, Dear?* by Sesyle Joslin.

67. *Crictor* by Tomi Ungerer.

68. Anatole, in the book *Anatole* by Eve Titus.

69. *The Fox Went Out on a Chilly Night* illustrated by Peter Spier.

70. *The Camel Who Took a Walk* by Jack Tworkov.

71. Mike Mulligan, in the book *Mike Mulligan and His Steam Shovel* by Virginia Lee Burton.

72. *Horton Hatches the Egg* by Dr. Seuss.

73. Curious George, in the book *Curious George Gets a Medal* by H. A. Rey.

74. Madeline, in the book *Madeline* by Ludwig Bemelmans.

75. *Song of the Swallows* by Leo Politi.

76. *I See the Winds* by Kazue Mizumura.

77. In both books mice try to bell a cat. Anatole succeeds, but in *Belling the Tiger* the bell is put on a tiger by mistake!

78. *Tikki Tikki Tembo* retold by Arlene Mosel.

79. *Where the Wild Things Are* by Maurice Sendak.

80. *A Pocketful of Cricket* by Rebecca Caudill.

81. *Fox and the Fire* by Miska Miles.

82. a) *Curious George* by H. A. Rey.
    b) *Make Way for Ducklings* by Robert McCloskey.
    c) *Fly High, Fly Low* by Don Freeman.

83. *Listen, Rabbit* by Aileen Fisher.

84. Tico, in the book *Tico and the Golden Wings* by Leo Lionni.

85. *Journey Cake, Ho!* by Ruth Sawyer.

86. Otto, in the book *Otto in Africa* by William Pène du Bois.

87. *Little Bear's Friend* by Else Holmelund Minarik.

88. *Look, There Is a Turtle Flying* by Janina Domanska.

89. Rosie, in *Rosie's Walk* by Pat Hutchins.

90. "Hansel and Gretel," in *Household Stories from the Brothers Grimm* translated by Lucy Crane.

91. Flip, in the book of that name by Wesley Dennis.

92. The cow jumped over the moon, in *The Hey Diddle Diddle Picture Book* by Randolph Caldecott.

93. Toys and candy for the boys and girls on the other side of the mountain.

94. He is the Tomten, in the book *The Tomten* adapted by Astrid Lindgren.

95. *Lucy McLockett* by Phyllis McGinley.

∼ II ∼

For Young Readers

Questions*

1. What book tells about a mischievous dog and the boy who owns him, and tells why the boy and the dog became known as the Pied Piper of Harlem?

2. Who brought his friends to see a mermaid that he thought his father would bring home from his fishing trip out in the ocean? The friends were Hen, Duck and Cat.

3. What book is this?
   a) A little boy is a stowaway on a ship.
   b) In a great storm the ship crashes on a rock.
   c) The captain and the boy are forgotten when the lifeboats leave the ship.

4. Who is the boy who couldn't sing or whistle, so he learned to play the harmonica? One day, when the town band was suddenly unable to play, he blew on his harmonica and saved the day.

5. What eight-year-old pioneer girl needed to be brave for long months, living in the forest with her father while he built a house in a new settlement? She had to be even braver when he had to go away, and left her with an Indian family.

6. In what fairy tale does a poor but greedy wife wish first for a cottage, then for a castle and power to be king, and finally, for the power to order the sun and the moon to rise?

7. In what book does a small boy walk a long distance to school every day for six years? He is always left alone by the other children, until the day in the sixth year when he performs at the talent show by imitating the voices of crows.

* See pages 42–47 for Section II answers.

8. In one of Aesop's fables, who taught us that "Slow and steady often wins the race"?

9. In what book about a house might you find a boy jumping and bumping on his bed, a rabbit eating a piece out of the door and a lion eating the stuffing from the chairs?

10. In what book does a boy of six, dressed as a shepherd in a striped robe and carrying a crook in one hand, run into church very early on Christmas morning with an orange and a dime?

11. Where would you be if you saw two bears sitting in the snow beside a large iron pot turned upside down with a boy hiding underneath it?

12. Who went to sea in a beautiful pea-green boat?

13. In what book does an animal draw a map on the bathroom floor with a tube of shaving cream, and then bail out the overflowing bathtub with his hat instead of pulling out the plug?

14. In what book does a raccoon persuade a goose to go for a walk in the woods so he can kill her, but every trick he tries to play on the goose backfires? The raccoon is stung by bees and bumped on the head, and a rock rolls on his paw.

15. Do you know the book in which a boy plays basketball wearing an underwater mask to protect his glasses because his mother refuses to allow him to buy any more sports equipment?

16. In the book *The Little House* by Virginia Lee Burton, what happened to the little house when the big city grew up around it and it couldn't see the sun and the moon because of the tall buildings?

17. A little girl with a big imagination often talks about her pet kangaroo. She doesn't really have one, but her friend Thomas thinks she does. One day she tells him to go out to Blue Rock to see her kangaroo, but after he leaves the tide comes in and a storm begins. Do you know this book?

18. Who is the animal who was supposed to be a fierce fighter, but liked to sit quietly under a cork tree and smell flowers?

19. In what book did the roadmaster worry about what people would say because the trains couldn't keep up with a long-legged, lop-eared hound?
    Clue: The hound's name is Sooner.

20. There are many books written about doll families. Can you identify two books by these descriptions?
    a) A doll family is shipwrecked on a tropical island, and the members have many adventures as they look for each other.
    b) A doll family loses all the men dolls: the father at a picnic, a brother given away to a little girl, and the littlest boy who fell out a window.

21. In what book does Jennie, a dog who has everything, leave her comfortable home because she thinks there must be more to life? She wants to act in a theater, but is turned away and told to get some experience. And she does!
    Clue: In one experience she saves a baby and herself from a lion.

22. In what book does a boy named Thaddeus collect empty bottles and newspapers because he wants to own a guitar?

23. In what book do men hunting animals for a zoo

find in one of their traps a huge bear and a little boy called Johnny?

24. In the book *Bright April* by Marguerite de Angeli, how did April win the prize in her Brownie troop, and what was it?

25. What family of brothers, each with a special craft, help their king find a beautiful princess to marry? When the king offers to give them high positions in court and all the gold and silver they need, they ask only to go back to their field to work.
    Clue: One brother can build a tall tall tower, and another can climb the tower and from the top see everything that goes on in all the world.

26. In the book *First Adventure* by Elizabeth Coatsworth, six-year-old Johnny wanders from the Plymouth settlement and is lost in the forest for five days until he comes to an Indian village. Why did the Indians of that village take him to another Indian village instead of taking him home?

27. Evan picks out a place in his family's two-room apartment, near a window, and paints a picture at school to hang there. One night he has dinner there all by himself. What does he call this place?

28. Out West in Indiana, Great-grandfather in only one day, with only one bullet, a bird net and an ax, brings home to Great-grandmother a barrel of wild honey, a bear, a large fish, a partridge, two-dozen geese, a deer and twelve wild turkeys, without really trying. What book tells this story?

29. Do you know the book in which a boy borrows a skunk from an animal lending library? Accidentally the skunk gets loose in school, runs into the prin-

cipal's office and jumps onto the desk, while the man sits *very* still because he doesn't know the skunk is harmless.

30. In what tale did a boastful father tell a king his daughter could spin gold out of straw?

31. Do you know the story of two boys who build a wagon to earn money by delivering groceries? They needed money because they had raced their coasters down a hill, nearly knocking people over and causing several things to be damaged.

32. In what story does a lonely orphan girl look in the window of a toy shop on Christmas Eve and see a doll wearing a red dress? "My Christmas doll!" the little girl says. The doll sees her and says, "My Christmas girl!" But a mean stuffed owl in the window says, "But the window is between."

33. In what book is Juan, a gaucho, or cowboy, fired because he tries to prevent the ranch owner's spoiled son from taking a colt that belongs to Pedro, a worker's son?

34. What tree, when offered as a reward a lantern that can light the night, a whip that can will the wind or a rod that can rule the rain, asked instead to be able to try to cure the princess, who was very ill? The tree knew that he would have to suffer much pain to do this.

35. In a book by Ann Nolan Clark, a little Navajo Indian girl fears the white man's school because Big Brother has gone to the school and stayed there to work. Now her older sister is going there, and she's afraid she won't come back. What book is it?

36. What boy in what book caused a king's carriage

to come to a halt and even back up because, un-
knowingly, the boy was wearing a hat before the
king?
Clue: Every time he took his hat off, another ap-
peared.

37. Whose house looked like this when Christmas
began? The carpet sweeper was on top of the piano,
a yellow silk sofa pillow was in the fireplace, cook
was lying on the kitchen floor and her wig was on
the clock, a frying pan lay on a bed, fireplace logs
were on top of a white dresser, a wooden Easter
egg was in the bathtub and nurse was standing
on her head in the bathroom sink.

38. In what collection of folk tales does a boy named
David singe the Devil's tail on the first night of
Hanukkah, because the Devil had kept his parents
from getting home?

39. A small lonely boy said one day:
    "I have no brothers and sisters. My mother had seven
    brothers and six sisters. She wasn't lonely, no? My
    father had four brothers and five sisters. And he had
    a friend . . . I'll go out and look for a friend."
    So the boy went to look for a friend, and he came
    home with a baby moose! Can you name this book?

40. Can you name the book in which a young boy finds
a man's wallet with fifteen hundred dollars in it?
When he returns the wallet, the owner, Mr. Thomp-
son, counts the money twice, then says, "Well, this
durn boy didn't steal any of it," and gives the boy a
nickel.
Clue: Another man saw this and made Mr. Thomp-
son give the boy two hundred dollars.

41. If you know Aesop's fables, then you know who
taught us:

a) A liar will not be believed even when he tells the truth.

b) Little friends may prove to be great friends.

42. In what Hans Christian Andersen tale did a ruler order some special cloth that, he was told, could only be seen by wise people and those who did their jobs well?

43. In the ancient country of Orn there lived an old man in a hut. One day a Junior Sorcerer stopped by and told him that he had been transformed from some other living thing. Immediately the old man set out to find his real self and be transformed back. Can you name this book?

44. Who spilled honey all over himself, then rolled in leaves hoping to get the honey off? Instead, he became a frightful sight and scared his worst enemies, a wolf and a fox.

45. A poor servant boy once sent his cat on a merchant voyage. When the ship returned the boy received a great fortune from a distant king and queen who bought the cat. Can you name the boy?

46. Who wore her hat to bed because she was afraid of a squirrel, and why?
Clue: Her home was a bird's nest.

47. Who is the girl who has let her best friend think she knows a lot about horseback riding, but when she has a chance to go riding with her friend, she finds she can't "steer" the horse, who is determined to stand in the middle of a swift stream?

48. Do you know the old tale of three hungry soldiers, coming home from war, who reach a village where no one will give them any food? So they promise to make the villagers a special kind of soup. First,

they say, they need a large iron pot, water and three smooth stones to put in the soup.

49. In what book does a boy on a rescue mission take with him chewing gum, twenty-four pink lollipops, rubber bands, black rubber boots, a compass, a toothbrush and toothpaste, six magnifying glasses, a very sharp jackknife, a comb and hairbrush, seven hair ribbons of different colors and an empty grain bag with a label reading "Cranberry"?

50. In what book are a tramp and a skunk locked in a railroad freight car where they travel uneasily together for several hours?

51. Twenty orphan girls living in an old dilapidated house, and a baby boy in the breadbasket, remind you of what book?

52. What book would you be in if a little girl, Minnikin Snickersnee, upset your school by arriving on her broomstick?

53. Two girls, identical twins, decide to write a story about an old doll they found in the attic—a mystery story in which the doll is stolen. When they take the doll to the park, she disappears and the twins learn she was a valuable heirloom. What book solves this mystery?

54. What is the name of the moose who was terribly hungry during a hard winter in Minnesota until he found a livery stable full of lovely hay?

55. What fairy tale do these three clues describe?
    a) Three brothers.
    b) Three golden apples.
    c) Three suits of armor: one brass, one silver and one gold.

56. Can you name the boy who was very pleased with his dog the day he trained him to bring in the newspaper, until the next morning, when he found seventeen papers on his doormat? And do you remember how he untrained his dog?

57. In what book does a little Mexican boy go to town for the first time because his mother receives a letter which no one in the family is able to read? He goes with an irresponsible uncle, and in town meets an uncle who is a poet.

58. In what book does a little country school raise money for library books by planning a cotton-picking picnic? All the parents and children who are able will pick cotton for half a day and donate their wages to the library fund.
    Clue: A girl named Joanda Hutley is very important in this book.

59. In what book does a mother, at night, slap an animal she thinks is her cow, then suddenly by the lantern light see that it is a bear?
    Clue: In the same book the father, walking home through the woods at night, sees what he thinks is a bear in his path. He hits it with a heavy branch because he doesn't have his gun, and he finds the "bear" is a tree stump.

60. When Annie Mae and Beanie Tatum took shelter in an old cabin during a rainstorm, who warned them that the creek was flooding?

61. In what book is a little girl, dressed in a brown snowsuit, mistaken for one of the seven dwarfs, so she is placed on a float and rides in the Santa Claus Parade?
    Clue: Sometimes this little girl is called Twinkle.

62. What schoolmaster had a horse so little that people laughed at it, until it won a pulling bee by pulling a log with three big men sitting on top?
Clue: Soon the horse Little Bub became famous for winning races, too.

63. In what story that took place about one hundred years ago are five girls taken to sea by their Aunt Hegarty because the girls believe their brothers always have the fun? The aunt, a determined explorer, tells them to bring clothes for danger. She buys an old steamer that had been a ferry, and they set out to sea. Their adventures include pirates, cannibals and diamonds.

64. If you saw a pet moose wearing sleigh bells and appearing as one of Santa's reindeer in a school Christmas play, of what book would you think?

65. In what book do two girls receive a present from a poor girl whom they had often teased about her clothes?
Clue: The present is a drawing of each of them wearing a pretty dress, which she sends after she has moved away to a big city.

66. In what story of postwar Paris does a hungry ten-year-old French boy go to the American embassy because he wants the American ambassador to translate the directions on a box of pancake mix given him by an American soldier?

67. In the story *Melindy's Medal* by Georgene Faulkner and John Becker, why did Melinda want so badly to win a medal, but was sure she couldn't because she was a girl?

68. In what book does Becky worry that there will not be ice cream for her eighth birthday? Becky's

mother works hard to support five children, but they are poor, and Becky's worries increase when she feels that her older sisters don't want her with them.

69. In what book is a boy, Shotaro, supposed to care for a baby fox that has been captured and chained by his father, but the little fox won't eat? One night Shotaro sees the parent foxes go into the shed where the captive is, and soon he knows that the parents have made their den close to their baby. Now he is afraid his father will shoot them.

70. When a black family moves into a white neighborhood and resentment toward the family arises, a small boy named Joey shows the neighborhood how wrong they are by disrupting the painting of a fence black on one side and white on the other. Name this book.

71. In the old Russian folk tale *My Mother Is the Most Beautiful Woman in the World* by Rebecca H. Reyher, a little girl is lost and looking for her mother. She tells people that her mother is the most beautiful woman in the world. When she finally finds her, why does her mother say, "I am grateful and lucky that you see with your heart, as well as with your eyes"?

72. What animal sat with his nose wrapped in banana leaves and resting in a river, waiting for it to shrink back to shape?
Clue: The river was the great-gray-green greasy Limpopo River.

73. In what book might you see a little cat sleeping between the paws of an old blind dog in a cage in a kennel?

74. In what book do a little girl, three aunts and two uncles travel from Massachusetts to Maine in a little house on runners?

75. Complete these titles with the name of a fruit. In both books a young boy is very important.
    a) *Little* ___ (by Eleanor Frances Lattimore).
    b) *The* ___ *and the Arrow* (by Mary and Conrad Buff).

76. What boy helps his father, the chief of police, solve crimes in the town of Idaville?

77. A dog named Sarge, a boy named Jeff, his sister Trudy, an abandoned shack and rescue by helicopter are all part of what book?

78. If you went to a dreary place called Shantytown, where there were old, broken-down houses and a junkyard, and met a small boy called Peter, a dog called Pal and a big policeman called Pat—then later you went there again and saw a garden, lots of grass, and houses repaired and painted, what book would you be in?

79. Can you name the book in which two girls, one in a Swedish costume, one in a Polish costume, ride to a picnic in a daisy chariot? The "chariot" is really a farm wagon which has been covered with daisies.

80. What boy and what two books do you think of when you hear of a parrot that was put in the wrong cage and traveled to another town three hundred miles from his owner, or a goat that got out of the baggage car on a train and broke open a pile of chicken crates?

81. What humorous detective story has policemen dressed as fish and thieves operating out of a boat that is disguised as a sea serpent?

82. When young Gluck poured the melted gold from the crucible, instead of a liquid stream out came a little golden dwarf. What book is this?

83. Lily Rose Ruggles, to surprise her mother who is a laundress, irons a customer's green silk petticoat. But she uses a hot iron and the garment shrinks to doll's size. What book is this?
    Clue: Lily Rose is a Girl Guide and has been trying to do her good deed for the day.

84. In what book are two little girls locked in a library at night, and later stuck at the top of a Ferris wheel that has stopped working?
    Clue: The girls' names are Garnet and Citronella.

85. A group of children get 419 signatures on a petition which they present to the mayor of their city in an attempt to change a rule against pets in the housing project in which they live. Name this book.
    Clue: They have been taking turns secretly feeding a pregnant cat.

86. In the book *Billy and Blaze* by C. W. Anderson, what animal did Billy find caught in a trap in the woods?

87. Do you know the French fairy tale of the duck who loaned the king one hundred pieces of silver? Luckily, when he set out to see the king to be repaid, some friends of his came along, for without these friends the duck would have had a hard time.
    Clue: The friends were a fox, a ladder, a river and a nest of wasps.

*A*nswers

1. *My Dog Rinty* by Ellen Tarry and Marie Hall Ets.

2. Little Bear, in *Father Bear Comes Home* by Else Holmelund Minarik.

3. *Little Tim and the Brave Sea Captain* by Edward Ardizzone.

4. The boy is Lentil, in the book of that name by Robert McCloskey.

5. Sarah Noble, in the book *The Courage of Sarah Noble* by Alice Dalgliesh.

6. "The Fisherman and His Wife," in *Grimm's Household Tales.*

7. *Crow Boy* by Taro Yashima.

8. The tortoise, as retold in the book *The Hare and the Tortoise,* illustrated by Paul Galdone.

9. *A Very Special House* by Ruth Krauss.

10. *A Certain Small Shepherd* by Rebecca Caudill.

11. On Hemlock Mountain, in the book *The Bears on Hemlock Mountain* by Alice Dalgliesh.

12. The owl and the pussycat, in the poem of that name in *The Complete Nonsense Book* by Edward Lear.

13. *A Bear Called Paddington* by Michael Bond.

14. *Petunia, I Love You* by Roger Duvoisin.

15. *Guards for Matt* by Beman Lord.

16. A lady, whose great-great-grandfather had built the

little house, had the house moved out on a hill in the country.

17. *Sam, Bangs, and Moonshine* by Evaline Ness.

18. A bull named Ferdinand, in *The Story of Ferdinand* by Munro Leaf.

19. *The Fast Sooner Hound* by Arna Bontemps and Jack Conroy.

20. a) *Floating Island* by Anne Parrish.
    b) *Home Is the Sailor* by Rumer Godden.

21. *Higglety Pigglety Pop! Or There Must Be More to Life* by Maurice Sendak.

22. *Song of the Empty Bottles* by Osmond Molarsky.

23. *The Biggest Bear* by Lynd Ward.

24. April identified the most birds and trees. The prize was a supper party at a farm with Brownies from other troops.

25. *Seven Simeons* by Boris Artzybasheff.

26. They were afraid that if they took him to Plymouth, or if Plymouth men came to the Indian village, they might be accused of kidnaping Johnny.

27. Evan's corner, in the book of that name by Elizabeth Starr Hill.

28. *Great-Grandfather in the Honey Tree* by Sam and Zoa Swayne.

29. *How to Read a Rabbit* by Jean Fritz.

30. "Rumpelstiltskin," from *Grimm's Fairy Tales*.

31. *Two Is a Team* by Lorraine and Jerrold Beim.

32. *The Story of Holly and Ivy* by Rumer Godden.

33. *Chúcaro, Wild Pony of the Pampa* by Francis Kalnay.

34. The Dwarf Pine Tree, in the book of that name by Betty Jean Lifton.

35. *Little Navajo Bluebird* by Ann Nolan Clark.

36. Bartholomew Cubbins, in *The 500 Hats of Bartholomew Cubbins* by Dr. Seuss.

37. Mr. and Mrs. Doll's house, in *Big Susan* by Elizabeth Orton Jones.

38. *Zlateh the Goat and Other Stories* by Isaac Bashevis Singer.

39. *My Friend Mac* by May McNeer and Lynd Ward.

40. *Farmer Boy* by Laura Ingalls Wilder.

41. a) The shepherd boy.
    b) The lion and the mouse.
    These characters are found in *Aesop's Fables* retold by Anne Terry White.

42. "The Emperor's New Clothes."

43. *The Bee-Man of Orn* by Frank R. Stockton.

44. Brother Rabbit, in "Brother Rabbit's Astonishing Prank" from *The Favorite Uncle Remus* by Joel Chandler Harris.

45. Dick Whittington, in "Whittington and His Cat" from *English Fairy Tales* collected by Joseph Jacobs.

46. Miss Hickory, in the book *Miss Hickory* by Carolyn Sherwin Bailey. Her body was a twig and her head

was a nut, and she was afraid the squirrel might want her head.

47. Ellen Tebbits, in *Ellen Tebbits* by Beverly Cleary.

48. *Stone Soup* by Marcia Brown.

49. *My Father's Dragon* by Ruth S. Gannett.

50. *Smoke Above the Lane* by Meindert DeJong.

51. *A Brother for the Orphelines* by Natalie Savage Carlson.

52. *Little Witch* by Anna Elizabeth Bennett.

53. *Missing Melinda* by Jacqueline Jackson.

54. Honk, in the book called *Honk, the Moose* by Phil Stong.

55. "Princess on the Glass Hill," from *East of the Sun and West of the Moon* by Peter C. Asbjörnsen and Jörgen I. Moe.

56. Henry Huggins in *Henry and Beezus* by Beverly Cleary. He untrained Ribsy with a water pistol.

57. *The Two Uncles of Pablo* by Harry Behn.

58. *Cotton in My Sack* by Lois Lenski.

59. *Little House in the Big Woods* by Laura Ingalls Wilder.

60. Beanie's puppy Tough Enough, in the book called *Tough Enough* by Ruth and Latrobe Carroll.

61. *Betsy's Little Star* by Carolyn Haywood.

62. Justin Morgan, in *Justin Morgan Had a Horse* by Marguerite Henry.

63. *The Cruise of the Happy-Go-Gay* by Ursula Moray Williams.

64. *Peter's Moose* by Hughie Call.

65. *The Hundred Dresses* by Eleanor Estes.

66. *Pancakes-Paris* by Claire Huchet Bishop.

67. Because her father had won a medal in World War I, and her grandfather had won one in the Spanish-American War, and her great-grandfather had won one in the Civil War.

68. *Striped Ice Cream* by Joan M. Lexau.

69. *The Golden Footprints* by Taro Yashima and Hatoju Muku.

70. *The Other Side of the Fence* by Molly Cone.

71. Because the mother is really big and fat and homely, but her little girl loves her and thinks she is the most beautiful woman in the world.

72. The elephant's child, in *Just So Stories* by Rudyard Kipling.

73. *The Last Little Cat* by Meindert DeJong.

74. *Away Goes Sally* by Elizabeth Coatsworth.

75. *Little Pear* and *The Apple and the Arrow*.

76. Encyclopedia Brown, in the book *Encyclopedia Brown, Boy Detective* by Donald J. Sobol.

77. *Two on an Island* by Bianca Bradbury.

78. *A Tree for Peter* by Kate Seredy.

79. *The Golden Name Day* by Jennie D. Lindquist.

80. Eddie, in *Eddie and Louella* (parrot) and *Eddie and Gardenia* (goat) by Carolyn Haywood.

81. *The Three Policemen* by William Pène du Bois.

82. *King of the Golden River* by John Ruskin.

83. *The Family from One End Street* by Eve Garnett.

84. *Thimble Summer* by Elizabeth Enright.

85. *Project Cat* by Nellie Burchardt.

86. A large dog. Billy called him Rex.

87. "Drakestail," from *Favorite Fairy Tales Told in France* retold by Virginia Haviland.

∾ III ∾

For Readers
in the Middle Years

Questions*

1. To what poor and hungry little girl was an attic skylight the way through which a secret friend brought her food, warm blankets and even furnishings and a fire for her cold bare room?

2. What young deaf boy built on a base of plywood an elaborate model village made almost entirely of used matchsticks and glue?
    Clue: An out-of-bounds ball from a cricket game destroyed a whole row of these houses and several weeks of the boy's work.

3. What boy wants an old printing press that a girl in his neighborhood has? He wants it so badly that he finally buys an old broken doll for ten cents and has a terrible time getting it home without his friends seeing him. Then his mother fixes the doll, and he trades it to the girl for the printing press.

4. Who had a horse called Widow Maker who once bucked a man so high he landed right on top of Pikes Peak?

5. Here is a fur cap. There is a peephole in front. A small animal might peek out to see what is going on. Now, here on the left side of the cap, a small animal *is* peeking out—no, he is leaning over the man who is wearing the cap. Now, who is wearing the cap, and who is whispering in his ear?

6. In what story does Emily, a girl on a farm, scrub a big white work horse with bleach, and even soak his fetlocks and tail in it, to impress her city cousin?
    Clue: The cousin who is coming to visit has written Emily about the book *Black Beauty.*

* See pages 82–91 for Section III answers.

7. Princess Irene had a ring which glowed like a fiery rose. When she was in danger she would put it under her pillow and follow an invisible thread that led from the ring to safety. What book is this?
    Clue: Her great-great-grandmother had given her the ring and had spun the thread from a particular kind of spider web.

8. In what story does a girl from an orphanage have to choose between being adopted by a lonely older woman or by a lively friendly family?

9. In an old folk tale a young prince must turn the manes and tails of four young colts to gold, or lose his life. And the next day he must turn the hoofs and horns of four young bullocks to gold. If you can name the animal that helped him, you will name the story.

10. In what book is a stuffed wildcat a means of passing messages among freedom workers on a Greek island?

11. When the Moon Maiden slips into the Black Men's Castle by night to try to arrange a truce, Monsieur Cocq de Noir demands a string of pearls that was lost hundreds of years before. What book is it?

12. In what story does a girl, who imagines she is heir to the throne of England, hide in the rumble seat of a Model-A Ford in an effort to save the car from new owners?
    Clue: The girl keeps a scrapbook of the British royal family. Her father is without a job.

13. Joey found a note on his mother's torn-up Christmas card, telling of his two brothers' great abilities, but describing him only as nice, normal and aver-

age. Each word felt like a knife wound. What book is this?

14. If one Halloween you dress up as an Indian, put a wolf mask on your dog and go out for trick or treat, who are you?
    Clue: At one house the lady has no treats, so she gives you a huge stuffed owl.

15. One night Zeke's mother held him in her lap a long time, teaching him to read and then rocking him to sleep, and he knew, deep down, that she wouldn't come home from work to him again. What story is this?
    Clue: Hour after hour this lonely boy watched other people from his window, and especially enjoyed watching and listening to a man play the piano.

16. In what book would you read this rule for table manners?
    "Every man is allowed both elbows and one knee on the table, but no more, so don't you try anything funny."

17. In what book would you find this unusual home described?
    "He built his house under a giant redwood tree. . . . He toted the biggest window he could buy to the cabin, and set it in the wall. . . . The window was as high as the wall; it was one wall as far across as the door. . . . The back wall was the redwood trunk. It made an odd house, one wall curved inward, and furnished with shaggy redwood bark."

18. What ten-year-old boy was sent to the top of a mountain to grow rice among the rocks because he was afraid to go fishing with the men and boys of his island? His father called him a coward.
    Clue: He is given only seven grains of rice to grow.

19. If your living room wallpaper was actually old letters placed sideways so the handwriting made vertical stripes from floor to ceiling, and the portraits on the wall were postage stamps, and you had a chest of drawers made of small matchboxes, who would you be? The answer is the title.

20. A young German boy and his friend spend their spare time treasure hunting in the ruins of bombed houses. They find a suitcase containing papers and a few valuable jewels, for which they receive a reward. The reward not only benefits them but, even more, benefits the many other refugees in the village. What book is it?

21. Walking over the grassy meadows once bloodied by the armies of the North and South, Jacob hears the Yankee bugler Hannibal calling the troops of the Second Maine. Later, Jacob rides with Colonel Ashby, and a stranger, dressed in black, speaks for peace. What book is this?

22. In what book do two boys, friends for years and rebel supporters during the Civil War, argue because the older brother of one joins the Union Army? To prove he's not a "blue-belly," the younger brother goes out at night and sets loose a whole pen full of Union supply mules.

23. What boy leaped aboard a Boston ship to apply for the job of cabin boy, but in standing on the deck he caused the ship to list dangerously?

24. A young boy and his baby sister sit before their burning house with a great Spanish gun in the boy's lap, their mother unconscious on the ground in front of them and three dead Indians nearby. Can you name this book?

25. Here are two clues to what book?
    a) A girl of eleven is known for telling unlikely stories.
    b) A retarded boy convinces her he has buried his parents in a swamp, after a rattlesnake had killed them.

26. A sullen "couldn't care less" city boy finds himself living in his great-uncle's shack on what island in the Tennessee River? The island has no electricity, no TV and no people, but has many large blue herons.
    Clue: He tries to catch one of these herons to collect a dollar bet from his uncle.

27. As this story opens a white rabbit hurries past a little girl. He takes a watch out of his tiny pocket and says, "Oh dear! Oh dear! I shall be too late!" What is the name of the book?

28. In Rumer Godden's book *Miss Happiness and Miss Flower*, why did Nona swap her two silver bracelets for Melly's wooden pencil box?
    Clue: The pencil box had a top of wood slats that rolled back when touched.

29. A girl named Rachel helps her brother earn money for a puppy by dusting the pews in church one Saturday. When she dusts the minister's pulpit she is inspired to give an imitation of a Sunday sermon. With a shock she sees the minister standing in the back of the church. What book is this?

30. Francie and Tony take over the care of a motherless black calf with an enormous appetite. When they enter their pet in the fat steer class, they don't realize that if he wins the blue ribbon he will also be judged "on the hook." What book is this?

31. In what general group of tales do you find a story in which the god of the underworld kidnaps the daughter of the goddess of harvest? While the mother searches for her daughter, nothing grows on the earth.

32. If you were to meet Mr. Toad of Toad Hall escaping from jail dressed as a woman, what book would you be in?
    Clue: You might also meet the Mole, the Rat or Mr. Badger.

33. In this tale of the Underground Railroad, a boy sees a Negro slave put zigzag cuts all over his back so he will fit the description on the papers of a dead Negro freedman. What book is it?
    Clue: This boy works as a hoggee for a canal boat captain.

34. If you came upon a cat and a pig discussing the clues to a crime, who might they be?
    Clue: The cat's name is Jinx.

35. A gang of ten children, searching for an important plaything that was stolen from them, find themselves in a pistol-and-firecracker battle with a gang of real bank robbers. What book is this?

36. Can you name the mystery which involves jewel thieves in London and a gang of children called the "Albry Street Syndicate"?

37. A group of children and a teacher are snowbound during a blizzard in a little schoolhouse in South Dakota. Two of the girls are arguing because their fathers forgot to bring coal and water to the teacher. The storm is fierce, and an Indian boy, woman and baby take refuge in the school, too. What book is this?

38. In the book *Heidi* by Johanna Spyri, why was Heidi saving white rolls from the dining table and keeping them in her room?

39. A twelve-year-old Hungarian boy flees his country, first in a boxcar, and then by crawling two hundred yards on his stomach in the dark through a minefield to cross the border into Austria. Can you name the book?
Clue: A horse had broken loose earlier that day and set off the mines, creating a narrow escapeway for the boy.

40. If you cut school one day and were kidnaped by three older boys who forced you to join in an illegal enterprise—"dog business incorporated"—you would be in what book?
Clue: You are forced to steal small dogs.

41. Mina, used to the warmth of Greece and unable to adjust to the cold, wet climate of Holland, goes for a lonely walk along the seashore and vanishes, leaving no trace, in what book?
Clue: Her brother Porphyras will not believe she is dead.

42. In what book does a pet cricket help improve the business at a family's newspaper stand?

43. In what book do a boy and a cricket become good friends? The cricket lives under the floor of the boy's room, and they learn to talk to each other in Morse code.

44. The day after Harry and Gerald meet Boadie, in the book *Crystal Mountain* by Belle Dorman Rugh, they go with her and her strange governess to Mystery House. Boadie finds a very queer window. What does it look out on?

45. If you were playing hide-and-seek in a house and suddenly found yourself in a snow-filled wood, where a lady riding in a sledge pulled by two white reindeer fed you a whole box of Turkish Delight, who would you be and in what book?
    Clue: The lady calls herself Queen, but she is really a witch.

46. In *Meet the Austins* by Madeleine L'Engle, when Uncle Doug called to say he was bringing a girl for a weekend visit, and he wanted all the family to behave very well, what did the Austin family do?

47. If you are a boy returning from your first trip to a cattle auction with gifts for your family, which your foster mother snatches away and destroys, what book tells your story?
    Clue: You live on the Isle of Skye during the depression years of the 1930s.

48. Jonathan Flower, the son of an American who has a secret government job, is lured by a false telegram away from the school he attends in Edinburgh, Scotland. He becomes involved in an exciting adventure that leads him back to his school and a gun battle there, in what book?

49. What lady led her sick cow out to pasture, and was astounded to see there a strange large contraption which turned out to be a spaceship about to leave Earth?

50. What girl is suspected of being a witch just because she did not drown when she jumped in the water to save a doll?

51. In what story does an animal called Tigger find that his favorite food is a baby kangaroo's Strengthening Medicine?

52. A young Japanese girl, Tomi Tomaki, returns with her family to Tokyo after it was bombed in 1945. The Tomakis live in a shack while a new home is being built, and Tomi wants most of all to have a room of her very own. What book tells her story?

53. In what collection of folk tales would you meet a pumpkin—not a coach turned into a pumpkin, but a pumpkin—rolling down the street with a beautiful girl imprisoned in it? Or you might meet a donkey who had convinced a lion that he was a lion tamer. Clue: Each of these tales begins with the words: "There was a time and there wasn't a time in the long ago. . . ."

54. What book tells the story of a war which began when a huge moving truck ran down a flower peddler's cart in New York City?
Clue: This event was later known in history as "The Daffodil Massacre."

55. In what book is a girl named Jane not quite happy with her place in the family, because when her mother introduces her children, she says, "my oldest child," "my oldest son," "the youngest in the family," but then just, "This is Jane"?

56. A spoiled, stormy city child named Kate visits her uncle's ranch and stirs up a lot of trouble. She starts his team of horses running away, goes swimming and is carried off by the current, and is taken away by the gypsies, in the book __ __ __.

57. If you are a boy named Mowgli, and your foster parents are wolves, what book tells your story?

58. A serf boy, Tomas, is given by his lord to a Jew as part payment of the lord's debt. What book is this?
Clue: This was done to punish the boy because he

had stolen a chicken from the lord's kitchen for his starving family, but Tomas finds his new master one to be loved and respected, rather than feared.

59. What gang of children waged a war in New York City against people they called the flots? The answer is the title.
Clue: In the gang you would meet C. C., Louise, Junior, Ivan and others.

60. What book do these clues describe?
a) Two children lost in a cave.
b) Three boys attending their own funeral.
c) Treasure bags of coins worth $12,000.

61. In a book of Indian legends, both Bear and Possum are tricked by other animals so that their tails are changed. Can you name the animals who tricked them, or can you name the book?

62. In what book does a boy gradually make friends with a bobcat by leaving fish on the ground below the tree where the huge cat rests?
Clue: The cat had saved the boy from an attack by a wild hog.

63. Lucinda was ten and, finally free of parents and her mam'selle, an "orphan" for a year in New York City. Her key to happiness and freedom is the title of this Newbery Medal book.

64. In what book does a family move from the South to Ohio, into a home which had been an important station in the Underground Railroad, and is reported to be haunted?
Clue: A boy named Thomas and an old caretaker named Pluto are important in the story.

65. In *The Witch's Daughter* by Nina Bawden, when

the jewel thief abandoned the children deep in the winding dark cave, how were they able to find their way out?

66. What story tells of a flier who makes a forced landing in the Sahara Desert? While he is trying to repair his engine, a small boy suddenly appears and asks him to draw a sheep.
Clue: Later the boy fears the sheep will eat something he values highly, so he asks the man to draw a muzzle.

67. What story of school integration has these three main characters?
   a) Lullah Royall, the only student still attending the recently integrated parochial school.
   b) Her older sister Emma, who is scrub girl at a motel.
   c) An ugly man called Mr. Buzzard, who came to stir up trouble.

68. A tidal wave is sweeping toward a little fishing village. On a hill above the village, a farmer holds a young boy to keep him from running down to the village to warn his family, because the farmer knows it is too late. What book is this?
Clue: The houses in the village face each other, and those beside the sea do not have windows facing the sea.

69. A Tory! How could the people of Woburn, Massachusetts, call her father that? The War for Independence was over thirty years ago, and anyway, her father just hadn't wanted to kill. Name this troubled family and the book about them.
Clue: Amity, the sixteen-year-old girl, had supported her family by working in a sail factory.

70. When his uncle dies in a wild night fire, Mark

Herron is released from a home which has been like a prison. Four motherless children adopt him as their brother, in what book?
Clue: The children are Mona, Rush, Randy and Oliver.

71. On the night of February 15, 1860, fourteen boys of the Chairman School in New Zealand board the schooner *Sloughie*. They are to start on a summer cruise the next day, but they wake up to find themselves adrift at sea. What book is this?

72. Larry Scott, an eleven-year-old orphan, finds himself liking Uncle Joe and Aunt Emma, his newest foster parents. But he tries not to like them too much, or the island where they live, because he believes that soon the state will find him a new home. What book is this?

73. In what book does a ten-year-old boy, who lives in Ancient Egypt, have fourteen copper rings that he had earned from the harvest of two fields given to him by his father?
Clue: He uses this money to buy a slave girl so she will not be separated from her family.

74. Two girls enter an essay contest—Maggie in the hope of winning an entry fee for her mare in the horse show, and Liz because she wants to buy a black satin gown for the junior prom. What book is this?

75. Tucker the housekeeper has an accident in London, and the four children left behind in the country must manage the house and themselves during their summer holiday on England's Cornish coast. Their parents are away, and no one in the town knows

that the children are alone. Can you name this book?
Clue: During the summer a valuable Chinese figurine is stolen by one of the children, who had learned to steal in a concentration camp.

76. Two boys, Clay and Paul, find a derelict boat, which each wants to claim. Clay is the son of black migrant workers, Paul is white and comes from a broken home. Warily they begin to work together to repair the boat. The name of the boat is in the title.

77. What family cut their own Christmas tree, but when they brought it in the house, they found it was too tall? So they raised the parlor ceiling, making a long hump in the floor of the bedroom above.

78. What girl, with her two brothers, held a "peep show" for their friends at which they showed an Indian scalp belt?
Clue: For admission, the children brought things like marbles, old birds' nests and slingshot crotches.

79. Mark Anderson's only friend was an Alaskan brown bear that Fog Benson kept chained in a dark rickety shed near Mark's route between school and home. This bear's name was what?
Clue: Mark buys the bear to save its life and tries to set it free, but the bear insists on staying with Mark and his family.

80. A boy, wearing pajamas, stands in a garden, teaching a little girl how to shoot a bow and arrow. Another day, in the same thin pajamas, he helps her build a tree house. And again, still in pajamas, he ice-skates with the girl. This happens in what book?
Clue: The girl's name is Hatty, and there is a grandfather clock that strikes thirteen.

81. In what book is a boy saving money so he can buy an old horse that belongs to a junkman, and a mixer for his mother who is ill? But he complicates his finances by using his mother's valuable rug to put out a fire.

82. What sixth grade girl is made terribly unhappy because of a notebook in which she has made notes about the people she knows and things she sees? Her classmates find the notebook and read what she has written about them.
    Clue: She keeps the notebook because she wants to be a writer.

83. In what book will you learn all about a sign that says:
    "Fresh Doughnuts, 2 for 5¢, while they last. $100 prize for finding a bracelet inside a doughnut. P.S. You have to give the bracelet back."

84. Lindy, wading in a dark cave in the sea wall, sees a green and brilliant circle of feathers which moves and glows in the water. She often goes back to see this strange object, in the book ___ ___ ___.

85. Willie is disappointed to find that Indians look like ordinary people and that no more scalpings occur out West, in Etowah, in 1905. At first he doesn't like the West and is determined to go back East, in what book?
    Clue: He sells candy to earn the $37.63 fare to take him back to Penn City, Pennsylvania.

86. On the first day of vacation a little girl writes her mother many postcards, dates them ahead for each day she is to be away and arranges for the cards to be mailed. Because of this, five lost children are not even missed by their families for eight days,

and not rescued for several more days, in the book ___.

87. What book tells of a man who, hundreds of years ago in Poland, from time to time scraped out the insides of a pumpkin, rubbed the shell with oils and gum to preserve it and then hid an object of great value within?
Clue: The object was known as the Great Tarnov Crystal.

88. Digory and Polly, exploring a palace in a strange, empty land, find a room with many still figures, and then see this verse cut in stone, in what book?
    "Make your choice, adventurous Stranger;
    Strike the bell and bide the danger,
    Or wonder, till it drives you mad,
    What would have followed if you had."

89. When Henny is half an hour late getting home one night, she persuades a friend to come with her so, maybe, her father won't spank her. When they climb the apartment stairs, all the lights are out and the door is locked. Henny tries to knock lightly on the wall to awake her sister. Instantly, the door opens, and before Henny can say a word her angry father puts her friend over his knee and gives her three hard spanks. Have you read this book?

90. Name two Newbery Medal books in which the ribs of a whale were life-saving to the leading character, and tell how they used them.

91. This boy's family moved constantly, following the crops, but he wanted to stay in one school long enough to learn "putting into." He knew that if you put three into ten, you got three, but wondered what to do with the number left over. Who was this boy?
Clue: His papa said to throw the leftover number

away, and his mama said to save it until you needed it.

92. Two English children and four American children become one family when an English widow marries an American widower. The children decide to call their joint father, Mr. Graham, "The Laird." What book is this?

93. A hunter lives alone on an island, where he and his parents had been shipwrecked years before. After his parents die he is lonely, until he makes friends with a mermaid. Then one day he brings home a bear cub. Gradually the family grows. Can you name this book?

94. In what book does a ten-year-old girl get revenge on her college brother by spreading rabbit scent all over their town in unlikely places? A fancy hunt the brother has planned for a group of college friends turns into a wild muddle with a pack of beagles roaring through people's yards.
Clue: She is mad at her brother because he does not want her around when he has his party.

95. The doctor explains to Meg that cerebral palsy occurs when a baby is born with a part of its brain's "motor" broken or injured, so that she may better understand her sister Sal's problems, in what book?

96. If you were a young boy asked to be the judge in a case concerning a jar of olives and a thousand pieces of gold, what story and book would you be in?

97. In the book *My Brother Stevie* by Eleanor Clymer, an older sister tries to keep her eight-year-old brother out of trouble in a crowded housing project in New York City. When a man catches Stevie

throwing rocks at a train, where does his sister turn for help?

98. When the Danes raided England, a one-legged boy longed to fight the enemy. Instead, he learned to write and became scribe to the king who brought peace to England. Can you name the book?
Clue: The boy's name was the same as that of the king.

99. Do you know the other name of a horse advertised as "The Cougar" who, during five years of rodeo work as a bucking horse, could throw any rider off his back? The horse's name is the name of a book.

100. What book are you reading if you find a small boy stealing twenty pounds of cabbage, broccoli, lettuce and beans in the middle of the night from his great-grandmother's garden, in order to feed one meal to a hidden animal?
Clue: The animal has escaped from a zoo.

101. What book are these events describing?
a) A house burning on Christmas night.
b) A young girl trying to get a meal for drunken lumberjacks.
c) A dishonest uncle.

102. If you were a boy named Tommy Stubbins, and you were talking with a duck named Dab-Dab, what book might you be in?

103. What little girl went to school just so she could have Christmas vacation? Before her first day was over she had drawn a life-size picture of her horse on the floor, and when the teacher asked her what seven and five are, she said, "Well, if you don't know that yourself, you needn't think I'm going to tell you."

104. In *Daughter of the Mountains* by Louise Rankin, a young Tibetan girl named Momo travels alone from Tibet to the coast of India, for what reason?

105. The only reward that Billy wanted was knowing that the Spaniards were safe from the outlaws and Indians. What book tells this legend?

106. If you read this newspaper headline, what book would you be reading: "Professor Sherman in Wrong Ocean with Too Many Balloons"?

107. In what book were two girls determined to run their motherless home without a housekeeper, and, if possible, find a wife for their professor father?
Clue: Keeping house was difficult, because father and some of his students were building a telescope in the living room.

108. What thirteen-year-old girl was afraid she was going to be sent to the reformatory because of a false accusation that she had broken the church windows? The answer is the title.
Clue: She is known to be the best stone thrower in the town.

109. In what book would you find this recipe for frog soup?

> "Clean, skin, and boil until tender. Add wild onions, also water lily bulbs and wild carrots. Thicken with acorn flour. Serve in a turtle shell."

110. In what book does a play about "The Flight into Egypt" become the real thing when a group of French children are asked to share their rationed food and beds with ten children who are being hunted by the Nazis?
Clue: Their teacher is put in jail, and two German soldiers arrive to search for the refugees.

111. Whose one room house, which he had made himself out of stone, had in it four bathtubs?
Clue: In these tubs he stored beets and cabbages, onions and potatoes, dust from sweeping out the churches and old newspapers.

112. The most pleasant room in the house was set apart for Beth when she became ill. In it was gathered everything that she most loved, and there Beth found a poem by her sister Jo, telling all Beth has meant to her and how she will miss her. Do you know this book?

113. Who would you be if you and your cousin come into an old decrepit house and find an elderly lady dressed in old-fashioned clothes? The lady's brother is sitting in the kitchen reading a very old newspaper. He says old news is more soothing to read about because you know you lived through it.
Clue: The house is on the edge of a swamp that was once a lake.

114. A thirteen-year-old boy sets out in India to take his seven-year-old sister to a very distant city where she might be saved from blindness. They are walking, and the trip is made more difficult by the false accusation that they have stolen a diamond ring from the moneylender's wife. What is the name of this book?
Clue: On the journey they are helped by a camel driver, and even given a ride on a maharajah's elephant.

115. Around a homemade temple in the backyard of a secondhand store, boys and girls perform a ceremony to the Oracle of Thoth—actually a stuffed owl—and write a question which they leave over-

night with the oracle. Twice when this is done, a member of the gang writes an answer on the back of the question. But the third time an answer appears, everyone is mystified, because no one in the gang had a chance to write it. Have you read ___ ___ ___?

116. Thirteen-year-old Tim has been sent to his aunt's ranch for the summer because his mother is very ill. At first he resents this. But he finds himself liking the place, and is drawn to a German shepherd dog who has roamed wild in the nearby mountains since his master was lost in an avalanche four years before. What book is this?
Clue: The dog's name is Lobo.

117. In what book does an eleven-year-old girl, who is spending the summer on her uncle's farm, convince herself and tell other children that a neighbor's daughter is a Watusi queen?
Clue: This "queen" lives with her mean-tempered father and helps raise razorback hogs.

118. Fideli promised Prince Perilous that if he could draw eyes, a nose and a mouth on the clock on the high church tower, he could have what reward? The reward is also the name of the book.
Clue: In another venture for the same reward, Prince Perilous tried to place an egg under the judge's mattress while the judge slept.

119. In what adventure story does an angry boy accidentally kick away a much needed flashlight, which leaves him and his companions in the dark in a dangerous situation?
Clue: The boys are on a narrow ledge in a cave far underground.

120. At a party for book characters, would you recognize this one? He is a round creature covered with thick close-cropped fur, possessing several retractable appendages such as eye stalks, and a tripod of bumps for locomotion. He has the unique ability of being able to repeat anything he hears in the voice tones of the original speaker.

121. At the same party, a tiny figure enters, walking very quietly on bare feet, wearing moleskin trousers and vest. He carries a hunting bow and a quiver made of a glove finger, filled with arrows made of pine needles tipped with black thorn. Who is he?

122. In what book would you see, by the light of a burning tree at night, an older boy digging frantically into an old mining tunnel in Australia? Suddenly his hands are on the shoes and legs of his little brother, trapped by a cave-in.
Clue: The younger boy was trying to earn money to help pay for their mother's operation.

123. Manolo Olivar looked like his father Juan, and everyone expected him to be a bullfighter as his father had been, in what book?

124. Two boys, Pony Rivers and Agba, each in a different book, travel great distances to be with a horse that each loves more than anything or anyone. Can you name the two books where you would meet these boys?

125. What do these three books have in common?
a) *Rain Forest* by Armstrong Sperry.
b) *Pinky Pye* by Eleanor Estes.
c) *Gull Number 737* by Jean George.

126. What is the name of the little wooden doll that Old

Peddler carved for a little girl, Phoebe Preble? The doll later wrote her memoirs with a quill pen.

127. Taran, a young man who lives in a remote corner of an unusual kingdom and longs to be a hero, suddenly finds himself involved in a hazardous, lengthy adventure, which begins when he chases a runaway pig into the forest. What book is this?

128. In what book would you find people who dressed alike in green cloaks, grew watercress and painted their doors green? Only a few rebels dared to have a red door, a yellow cloak, or an orange sash.

129. In what book are four children befriended by a kind old gentleman who helps the oldest boy learn about the forest and even offers to help solve their aunt's financial problems? But the children work against the man's ambition, which is to catch a certain fox. Clue: The aunt rents an old mill house from the gentleman.

130. In what book does a burning airplane explode on an Austrian mountain and start a tremendous avalanche, which imprisons a lame man and his twin grandsons in a farmhouse?

131. After World War II a nine-year-old refugee from Hungary arrives in this country. He is called Michael Prince, because no one believes him when he gives his real name. His only possession is an acorn in a little bag, worn on a string around his neck. Can you name the book and tell the boy's real name?

132. What man built a raft and made twelve trips between a wrecked ship and an island, salvaging everything he could use for his survival?

133. In what book are sixteen-year-old twins, a boy and a girl, stormbound in a small cabin in a desolate bay in Alaska? Their two older brothers had left in the family's steamboat to take a desperately ill younger brother to a doctor.

134. In each of these books a brother and a sister run away. From these descriptions, can you name the two books?
    a) A brother and sister run away from a cruel uncle in London to try to find a grandmother who, they remember, lives "somewhere in the West of Ireland." When the children become heirs to a legacy, the uncle pursues them, aided by police.
    b) A brother and sister leave their comfortable home and hide in the Metropolitan Museum of Art in New York City.

135. What dog story do these clues describe?
    a) A headstrong, unmanageable puppy.
    b) An injured boy out in the woods in a storm.
    c) A puma trying to kill the pup.

136. A warrant is out for Sir Patrick Hume's arrest, and his twelve-year-old daughter must hide him from the English troops. On another occasion, she is entrusted with the dangerous mission of delivering a letter to Robert Baillie in Tollbooth Prison. Name this book.

137. In what book does a boy named Martin, who is often in trouble, burn his shoes and his friend's shoes while trying to dry them in the oven after playing in the snow? He lends his friend his father's galoshes to wear home, and the following morning

Martin's father has to wear his fishing boots to wade through three feet of snow to the car.

138. Three children drift ashore on a strange island. At first the inhabitants are very frightened, then they become very kind, until the youngest boy plays with the Ferris wheel in the amusement park and puts a police sergeant and his car on top of the roller-skating palace! Have you read this book?

139. What book tells the story of a superb black horse, loved and cherished, then misused and ill-treated, who finally comes back to good hands and kind owners, and to the groom Joe Green?
Clue: Joe Green had once almost killed this same horse when he was an inexperienced groom's helper.

140. In what book does a boy risk his life to stop runaway horses which had bolted when a poisonous snake dropped from the sky and landed on the driver's head?
Clue: A kookaburra had caught the snake and flown up high in the sky, then dropped it to kill it.

141. In some books animals do unusual things. From the descriptions can you name these two books?
a) A burro wears trouser legs on his front legs, held up by suspenders.
b) A rat ties a string to a pig's tail.

142. In this story an Indian boy learns an important lesson—that slavery, rather than the slave, is to be despised—when three Spaniards and a Negro slave take him to Mexico. What book is this?
Clue: At one point the group pretends the slave has been bitten by a rattlesnake so that they can stay with Indians to rest and be fed.

143. Do you know the story and the book where a boy

named Jack fools a two-headed giant by pretending to squeeze milk out of a stone? Later he fools a four-headed giant by threatening to move the creek up to the house so he won't have to carry two huge buckets of water.

144. Can you name two books by English authors in which a group of children have wonderful adventures because a boy teaches them to fly?

145. A little old woman said to a little girl, "You are welcome to the land of the Munchkins." In what book does this happen?

146. Kelpie, a girl raised by the gypsies, believed she had been stolen by them when she was a baby, because of her blue-ringed eyes which the gypsies believed to be a sign of second sight. But the people of Inverness, Scotland, believed she was a witch and wished to burn her. Name this book.

147. In what book do two boys go off on a raft down the Wisconsin River, hunting lost treasure? Instead of finding treasure they find a hideout in a cave and are kept prisoners there by two men.
Clue: The two men are counterfeiters.

148. What girl moves with her family, by covered wagon, from Kansas to Minnesota because her father wants to farm wheat? But before he can harvest his first crop and pay their debts, millions and millions of grasshoppers come and destroy all the wheat for miles around.

149. In what book did a young orphan boy travel by train for two days with a baggage check tied on his shirt? No matter how warm he was, he kept his coat on to hide the check.
Clue: Part of the title is a part of a gun.

150. In what book does a man, walking home on a dark night, offer to help three men who are struggling to carry a heavy coffin up a hill? When they reach the graveyard the moon comes out, and he sees that his companions are three brothers, former neighbors of his, all of whom had drowned the year before.

151. An old tunnel leading to an old abandoned church, a gang of children, thieves on the church roof and a man who had been a corporal in World War I are all part of the book ___ ___ ___ ___ ___ ___.

152. In what book would you read of these events?
    a) A large wooden crate arriving by air express from Antarctica.
    b) A man paying five dollars to have holes drilled through his refrigerator door?

153. Eleven-year-old Merca and her little brother Dag are saved from death at the hands of King Malcolm's Scottish soldiers. But they are sold into slavery, where they labor for a cruel mistress, until at last they make plans for escape. What book tells this story?

154. What book would you be in if you saw:
    a) A boy hanging onto a hayloft door frame, with a rope pulling down from his waist and a heavy wheel swinging at the end of the rope.
    b) Another boy rolling a bright and shiny red, white and blue wheel over to a poor tinman's wagon, and trading the new wheel for an old broken wheel.
    c) An old man and a little girl sitting on an old overturned boat, with the tide rushing in around them, but happy because they have found a wheel under the boat.

155. Whose gun was carried at the famous battle of the Plains of Abraham under General Wolfe, then placed on a bracket over the fireplace for ten years? It was never to be taken down again, except to defend king and country.
Clue: It was taken down and raised to fire *against* the king in the Battle of Bunker Hill.

156. In what story does a girl named Ellen take part in a crime in New York City without knowing it? She also helps on the playground of her apartment project on long summer days.

157. In what book is a young teen-age boy, a crop picker who has no name and no family, befriended by a girl and her family of migrant workers? The boy lives and travels with the family, until a tragic accident occurs. Then he goes off on his own, and it is many months before he has a name.

158. What book tells of a girl who, aided only by an old servant, one settler and two militiamen, defended a fort for a week against an Indian attack?
Clue: A pumpkin head on a stick, topped by a soldier's hat with a cock's feather, was used to draw the Indians' fire.

159. In what book does a pink whale help destroy a plot to shoot a huge cannonball from Nantucket Island to London?

160. In what story do two orphans, Emily and her brother Toby, have many adventures, including chases by revenue agents and wrecks at sea, aboard an old fishing smack which had been left them by their father?
Clue: Emily is employed as a maid in a fine home on the Essex seacoast.

161. In what book does a young boy, Rudi, join an Englishman's climbing expedition in order to plant on the summit of the mountain a red shirt worn by his father on his last climb?
Clue: Rudi's father had frozen to death on that same mountain rather than desert an injured companion.

162. In what book does a father, who is separated from his wife, take his son David deep into a national forest on a camping weekend? The boy is afraid of his father, and the father worries that the boy is going to grow up a sissy, so he plans a rugged trip.
Clue: A huge animal, not in the father's plans, turns the weekend into a near tragedy.

163. A diamond palace, a mean, ugly duchess, twelve mechanical ladies-in-waiting and a thin little kidnaped orphan girl who is treated cruelly, are all part of what story?

164. In this Civil War story, a young Union scout escapes from the Confederates, but is pursued by a renowned Texas bloodhound. Surprisingly, the scout coaxes the hound to be his friend. What book is it?

165. In what book do a girl and a boy accidentally start a gold rush in California by pretending they had found a gold nugget in a stream? Actually, the nugget was a souvenir from Chinatown and was worn on a bracelet.

166. Two boys go out at night to find a candle which is the only proof of a strange visitor from an earlier century. They find the candle still burning and unconsumed twenty-four hours later. The flame burns

cold and will not be blown out. This happens in what book?

167. A crippled boy slips through a door of a besieged English castle, and on his crutches hobbles down a deep ravine to the river, which he must swim if he is to get help. The boy's name is Robin. What is the name of the book?

168. Can you identify this book?
   a) A lighthouse with a missing keeper and a lamp that will not light.
   b) An island on which the trees and boulders move.
   c) A pool with a deep center called "The Unfathomable Depths."

169. Three people approached a domed building on a strange planet. They were sucked inside, and there on the dais lay a most revolting thing—a disembodied, oversized brain that pulsed and quivered, seized and commanded. What book is it?

170. Jim and Larry are walking toward their old, overcrowded school in a dirty dreary part of town. Larry says:
   "Well, if it isn't the old school building, still standing, crutches and all. You can hear her getting ready to die. She can't breathe, and her head is splitting but she's got no aspirins. One of these days we'll come here and . . . we'll see a big pile of bricks and dust."
   Jim's mother protests, and soon Jim and his classmates are going to another school in a better part of town. But Larry won't go. He stays in the __ __ __ (also the title of the book).

171. If you were a fourteen-year-old boy sent to Maine

to live with your stubborn old grandfather and work on his farm, so you wouldn't have to go to reform school in Massachusetts, who would you be?

172. Can you name these two books?
    a) In one, five children have adventures after they wish on a book.
    b) In the other, four children order magic from a turtle.

173. In what book do young Sarah and Kevin, living in a new neighborhood with their always unreliable and occasionally dishonest uncle, attempt to manage the family's problems, which begin with a van load of unwanted new furniture and a department store owner's suspicious business operations?

174. A ten-year-old boy has helped an English flier who was shot down over Holland during World War II. One night, a neighbor who spies for the Germans chases the boy. To escape, he jumps onto the moving wing of a windmill and disappears. What book is this?

175. Two mice have many adventures as they search for an elephant, a seal and a home. They are involved in an attempted bank robbery, join a group of actors briefly, have their fortunes told by a frog and are pursued by an angry rat. What book is this?
    Clue: The two mice had once, when wound up, danced under a Christmas tree.

176. David Moss stared. A real boat, and right at his own dock. It was a brown canoe and looked very old. Later, David and the owner of the boat, Adam Codling, spend the summer searching for the Cod-

ling family treasure which had been buried in the sixteenth century. Name the canoe and the book.

177. Can you name these two tall tales by William Owen Steele?
     a) In one, a famous American goes off to help the people of Nashville, who are suffering from a serious drought, and brings back a well.
     b) In another, a famous frontiersman goes hunting for bears in 1811 and finds some, but he also must struggle with a comet and an earthquake.

178. In the book *The Trail of the Hunter's Horn* by Billy C. Clark, what is the purpose of the horn which Uncle Jeptha gives his nephew?

179. In what book do four thieves stop a horse and buggy at night and take the driver's wallet and gold watch? The thieves return the stolen goods when the leader recognizes the man as the doctor who saved his wife's life.
     Clue: The doctor's son is the other passenger in the buggy.

180. A very tiny boy is being hunted by a fox, but one night he tricks the fox and leaves him chained to a dog's kennel. A month later, the same boy finds the fox in a zoo and helps him to freedom. The boy's name is part of the title.
     Clue: The boy has been living with wild geese for several weeks.

Answers

1. Sara Crewe, in *A Little Princess* by Frances Hodgson Burnett.

2. David, in *David in Silence* by Veronica Robinson.

3. Eddie, in *Eddie and His Big Deals* by Carolyn Haywood.

4. Pecos Bill, in *Pecos Bill: The Greatest Cowboy of All Time* by James Bowman.

5. Ben Franklin is wearing the cap, and Amos the mouse is whispering in his ear, in the book *Ben and Me* by Robert Lawson.

6. *Emily's Runaway Imagination* by Beverly Cleary.

7. *The Princess and the Goblin* by George Macdonald.

8. *Adopted Jane* by Helen F. Daringer.

9. "The Golden Lynx," from *The Golden Lynx and Other Tales*, selected by Augusta Baker.

10. *Wildcat Under Glass* by Alki Zei.

11. *The Little White Horse* by Elizabeth Goudge.

12. *The Majesty of Grace* by Jane Langton.

13. *The Year of the Raccoon* by Lee Kingman.

14. Henry Huggins, in *Henry and the Clubhouse* by Beverly Cleary.

15. *The Jazz Man* by Mary Hays Weik.

16. *Good Old Archibald* by Ethelyn M. Parkinson.

17. *Kildee House* by Rutherford Montgomery.

18. Li Lun, in *Li Lun, Lad of Courage* by Carolyn Treffinger.

19. *The Borrowers* by Mary Norton.

20. *The Ark* by Margot Benary-Isbert.

21. *The Spring Rider* by John Lawson.

22. *The Perilous Road* by William Owen Steele.

23. Alfred Bulltop Stormalong, in the book *Mister Stormalong* by Ann Malcolmson and Dell J. McCormick.

24. *The Matchlock Gun* by Walter D. Edmonds.

25. *Ellen Grae* by Vera and Bill Cleaver.

26. Big Blue Island, in the book of that name by Wilson Gage.

27. *Alice's Adventures in Wonderland* by Lewis Carroll.

28. Nona wanted the box for a cupboard in her Japanese dollhouse.

29. *Ginger Pye* by Eleanor Estes.

30. *Birkin* by Joan Phipson.

31. Greek mythology, as found in the *D'Aulaires' Book of Greek Myths* (and other collections).

32. *The Wind in the Willows* by Kenneth Grahame.

33. *Canalboat to Freedom* by Thomas Fall.

34. Freddy the pig and Jinx the cat, in *Freddy, the Detective* by Walter R. Brooks.

35. *The Horse Without a Head* by Paul Berna.

36. *A Saturday in Pudney* by Roy Brown.

37. *Prairie School* by Lois Lenski.

38. The soft white rolls were for Peter's grandmother who could not eat hard black bread.

39. *Dangerous Journey* by László Hámori.

40. *How Many Miles to Babylon?* by Paula Fox.

41. *The Orphans of Simitra* by Paul-Jacques Bonzon.

42. *The Cricket in Times Square* by George Selden.

43. *The Cricket Winter* by Felice Holman.

44. The window looked out on nothing.

45. Edmund, in *The Lion, the Witch and the Wardrobe* by C. S. Lewis.

46. They all went to meet his train dressed in funny clothes, and Daddy pretended to be the chauffeur.

47. *The Rough Road* by Margaret M. MacPherson.

48. *Guns in the Heather* by Lockhart Amerman.

49. Miss Pickerell, in *Miss Pickerell Goes to Mars* by Ellen MacGregor.

50. Kit Tyler, in *The Witch of Blackbird Pond* by Elizabeth George Speare.

51. *The House at Pooh Corner* by A. A. Milne.

52. *The Cheerful Heart* by Elizabeth Janet Gray.

53. *Persian Folk and Fairy Tales* by Anne Sinclair Mehdevi.

54. *The Pushcart War* by Jean Merrill.

55. *The Middle Moffat* by Eleanor Estes.

56. *The Good Master* by Kate Seredy.

57. *The Jungle Book* by Rudyard Kipling.

58. *A Boy of Old Prague* by Sulamith Ish-Kishor.

59. *The Seventeenth-Street Gang* by Emily Cheney Neville.

60. *The Adventures of Tom Sawyer* by Mark Twain.

61. Fox tricked Bear. Raccoon tricked Possum. The book is *The Long-Tailed Bear and Other Indian Legends* by Natalia M. Belting.

62. *The Wahoo Bobcat* by Joseph Wharton Lippincott.

63. *Roller Skates* by Ruth Sawyer.

64. *The House of Dies Drear* by Virginia Hamilton.

65. One of the children, Janey, was blind, and with her good memory and ability to get around in the dark she led them out.

66. *The Little Prince* by Antoine de Saint-Exupéry.

67. *The Empty Schoolhouse* by Natalie Savage Carlson.

68. *The Big Wave* by Pearl S. Buck.

69. The Lyte family, in *The Limner's Daughter* by Mary Stetson Clarke.

70. *Then There Were Five* by Elizabeth Enright.

71. *A Long Vacation* by Jules Verne.

72. *Star Island Boy* by Louise Dickinson Rich.

73. *Boy of the Pyramids* by Ruth Fosdick Jones.

74. *Dark Horse of Woodfield* by Florence Hightower.

75. *A Poppy in the Corn* by Stella Weaver.

76. *Sail, Calypso* by Adrienne Jones.

77. The Peterkins, in *The Peterkin Papers* by Lucretia P. Hale.

78. Caddie Woodlawn, in the book of that name by Carol Ryrie Brink.

79. Ben, in the book called *Gentle Ben* by Walt Morey.

80. *Tom's Midnight Garden* by Philippa Pearce.

81. *Mr. De Luca's Horse* by Marjorie Paradis

82. *Harriet the Spy* by Louise Fitzhugh.

83. *Homer Price* by Robert McCloskey.

84. *The Feather Star* by Patricia Wrightson.

85. *Willie and the Wildcat Well* by Alberta Wilson Constant.

86. *Landslide* by Véronique Day.

87. *The Trumpeter of Krakow* by Eric P. Kelly.

88. *The Magician's Nephew* by C. S. Lewis.

89. *More All-of-a-Kind Family* by Sydney Taylor.

90. a) In *Island of the Blue Dolphins* by Scott O'Dell, Karana made a fence of whale ribs and kelp to keep away the wild dogs.
    b) In *Call It Courage* by Armstrong Sperry, Mafatu made a knife, ax and other tools of whale ribs.

91. Roosevelt Grady in the book of that name by Louisa R. Shotwell.

92. *Storm from the West* by Barbara Willard.

93. *The Animal Family* by Randall Jarrell.

94. *Edie on the Warpath* by E. C. Spykman.

95. *Mine for Keeps* by Jean Little.

96. "Ali Cogia, Merchant of Bagdad," from *Arabian Nights* edited by Andrew Lang.

97. She goes to Miss Stover, Stevie's teacher.

98. *The Namesake: A Story of King Alfred* by C. Walter Hodges.

99. Smoky, in the book *Smoky, the Cowhorse* by Will James.

100. *A Stranger at Green Knowe* by Lucy M. Boston.

101. *The Taste of Spruce Gum* by Jacqueline Jackson.

102. It could be any of the Doctor Dolittle books by Hugh Lofting.

103. Pippi Longstocking, in the book of that name by Astrid Lindgren.

104. A wool merchant has stolen her red-gold Lhasa apso terrier to sell to an English lady in Calcutta. Momo goes after him to get her dog.

105. *The Legend of Billy Bluesage* by Jonreed Lauritzen.

106. *The Twenty-One Balloons* by William Pène du Bois.

107. *Those Miller Girls!*, by Alberta Wilson Constant.

108. *Queenie Peavy* by Robert Burch.

109. *My Side of the Mountain* by Jean George.

110. *Twenty and Ten* by Claire Huchet Bishop.

111. Onion John's house, in *Onion John* by Joseph Krumgold.

112. *Little Women* by Louisa May Alcott.

113. Julian and Portia, in *Gone-Away Lake* by Elizabeth Enright.

114. *The Road to Agra* by Aimée Sommerfelt.

115. *The Egypt Game* by Zilpha Keatley Snyder.

116. *The High Pasture* by Ruth Harnden.

117. *Zeely* by Virginia Hamilton.

118. *The White Stone* by Gunnel Linde.

119. *Five Boys in a Cave* by Richard Church.

120. Willis, in *Red Planet* by Robert A. Heinlein.

121. Spiller, in *The Borrowers Afield* by Mary Norton.

122. *The Family Conspiracy* by Joan Phipson.

123. *Shadow of a Bull* by Maia Wojciechowska.

124. Pony Rivers, in *Little Vic* by Doris Gates. Agba, in *King of the Wind* by Marguerite Henry.

125. In each book, the father is an ornithologist, a scientist who studies birds.

126. Hitty, in the book *Hitty, Her First Hundred Years* by Rachel Field.

127. *The Book of Three* by Lloyd Alexander.

128. *The Gammage Cup* by Carol Kendall.

129. *Old One-Toe* by Michel-Aimé Baudouy.

130. *Prisoners in the Snow* by Arthur Catherall.

131. *The Chestry Oak* by Kate Seredy. The boy's real name was Michael, Prince of Chestry.

132. Robinson Crusoe in the book of that name by Daniel Defoe.

133. *Watch for a Tall White Sail* by Margaret E. Bell.

134. a) *The Flight of the Doves* by Walter Macken.
     b) *From the Mixed-Up Files of Mrs. Basil E. Frank-weiler* by E. L. Konigsburg.

135. *Irish Red* by Jim Kjelgaard.

136. *Story of Grizel* by Elizabeth Kyle.

137. *The Bully of Barkham Street* by Mary Stolz.

138. *Castaways in Lilliput* by Henry Winterfeld.

139. *Black Beauty* by Anna Sewell.

140. *Rain Comes to Yamboorah* by Reginald Ottley.

141. a) *Brighty of the Grand Canyon* by Marguerite Henry.
     b) *Charlotte's Web* by E. B. White.

142. *Walk the World's Rim* by Betty Baker.

143. "Jack in the Giants' Newground," from *Jack Tales: Folk Tales from the Southern Appalachians*, collected by Richard Chase.

144. *Peter Pan* by James M. Barrie and *The Summer Birds* by Penelope Farmer.

145. *The Wizard of Oz* by L. Frank Baum.

146. *Witch of the Glens* by Sally Watson.

147. *The Moon Tenders* by August Derleth.

148. Laura Ingalls, in *On the Banks of Plum Creek* by Laura Ingalls Wilder.

149. *Trigger John's Son* by Tom Robinson.

150. *Ghosts Go Haunting* by Sorche Nic Leodhas.

151. *The Battle of St. George Without* by Janet McNeill.

152. *Mr. Popper's Penguins* by Richard and Florence Atwater.

153. *The Queen's Blessing* by Madeleine Polland.

154. *The Wheel on the School* by Meindert DeJong.

155. John Treegate's musket, in the book of that name by Leonard Wibberley.

156. *Ellen and the Gang* by Frieda Friedman.

157. *The Loner* by Ester Wier.

158. *Madeleine Takes Command* by Ethel C. Brill.

159. *Nightbirds on Nantucket* by Joan Aiken.

160. *The Maplin Bird* by K. M. Peyton.

161. *Banner in the Sky* by James Ramsey Ullman.

162. *The Grizzly* by Annabel and Edgar Johnson.

163. *Miss Bianca* by Margery Sharp.

164. *Rifles for Watie* by Harold Keith.

165. *Henry Reed's Journey* by Keith Robertson.

166. *Earthfasts* by William Mayne.

167. *The Door in the Wall* by Marguerite de Angeli.

168. *Moominpappa at Sea* by Tove Jansson.

169. *A Wrinkle in Time* by Madeleine L'Engle.

170. *Dead End School* by Robert Coles.

171. Ralph, in *The Fields of Home* by Ralph Moody.

172. a) *Seven-Day Magic* by Edward Eager.
     b) *Magic by the Lake* by Edward Eager.

173. *Good-Bye to the Jungle* by John Rowe Townsend.

174. *The Winged Watchman* by Hilda van Stockum.

175. *The Mouse and His Child* by Russell Hoban.

176. The canoe is called *Minnow*, in *The Minnow Leads to Treasure* by Philippa Pearce.

177. a) *Andy Jackson's Water Well.*
     b) *Davy Crockett's Earthquake.*

178. It is a hunter's horn and is the only thing that will break a good hound from the trail, even if he is in sight of game.

179. *Doctor's Boy* by Karin Anckarsvärd.

180. *The Wonderful Adventures of Nils* by Selma Lagerlöf.

～ IV ～

For Older Readers

Questions *

1. Bored with cleaning the family cellar, Peter Griswold drives to the nearby beach on Long Island Sound and takes a walk. He sees an empty car, a strange boat, and then a dead lobsterman floating near some rocks. Within minutes he is being chased by a man who fires two shots at him. What book is this?

2. In what book does this idea begin the integration of an all-Negro school?
   " 'Well, why don't we go to the new school?' Carla's eyes were wide with surprise at the startling simplicity of her suggestion. 'Why don't we just go?' "

3. In what book does a medallion, decorated with the figure of a dolphin holding a lily in its mouth, help a girl who is tormented by the sudden knowledge that she is adopted?
   Clue: The girl, Willow Forrester, hopes to be a concert pianist, though her parents don't feel music is very important.

4. In what book does a poor widow with her six children move from Colorado to Massachusetts so she will not be forced to testify in court against a friend? She struggles to support her family in the new town by doing fancy hand laundry in her home.
   Clue: Her son, who was used to riding horses, gets a new job riding a bicycle to deliver groceries.

5. Two hundred years ago, a young bound-out girl lives in New England with a family that does not celebrate Christmas. On Christmas Eve she is frightened when an Indian steps out of the woods near her, but impulsively she gives him one of her

* See pages 110–114 for Section IV answers.

two treasures, a gilt button that had belonged to her uncle. Can you name the book?

6. The final test for the championship of Ireland required the warrior to lay his head on the block, ready to have it cut off by the executioner. Only Cuchulain passed the test. What book tells of this?

7. Can you name the Newbery Medal book which tells of a high school girl who lives with her strict but kind aunt? The girl secretly wants to be a writer, but because her jobless, alcoholic uncle always claims to be writing a book, she doesn't want to speak of her ambition.

8. In what book does a family move from the city to a flower farm in the country? Their nearest neighbor, Mr. Tower, resents them, and bad luck comes again and again. Then the son is accused of stealing a beautiful weather vane from Mr. Tower.

9. In what book by Jim Kjelgaard is a young cave man run out of his tribe because the weapons he makes are far superior to those his tribe uses, and the men are suspicious of him?

10. What twelve-year-old boy made these preparations for Christmas? After decorating a tree in the living room bay window, he screened off the area with chicken wire, then laced Christmas ribbons through the ribs of the canoe he was building in the living room.

11. An abandoned subway station in New York becomes the secret headquarters for a power-mad fanatic and his sinister followers in the book ___ ___ ___.

12. If you saw a map with these places identified on it, could you name the land about which the map tells,

or could you name some books in which you would read of these places: Lantern Waste, Archenland, Calormen, Caldron Pool, Cair Paravel?

13. A baby girl is chosen to be the future wife of a king. As she grows up the king worries that she will fall in love with a younger man than he. So for seven years he has her imprisoned in a walled-in house, far in the forest, with two servants for companions. Can you name this book?

14. What fifteen-year-old boy worked out a survey to take around to neighbors so he could plan a way to earn money for the summer? He asked people if they wanted their lawns mowed regularly, or had horses that needed exercising, or would like their cars washed each week. He was dismayed to have the greatest number of people say they needed baby-sitters.

15. In what book does a plane crash bring together a boy and an injured dog? The dog was raised to be a champion sled dog, and until his rescue by the boy had never known love or gentleness.

16. Three refugee children make their way on foot from Naples to Cassino in war-torn Italy. On the way they are held captive by a thief, befriended by peasants, fired on by soldiers and almost always hungry. Can you name this book?

17. What book tells the story of the young shepherd Nicholos, in Greece during the days of civil war, who with his sister Angela and all the children of his village is kidnaped by the Andarte, the Communist partisan fighters?
Clue: His sister leaves the children and joins the Andarte, while the rest try to escape.

18. What is similar in the two books, *Johnny Tremain* by Esther Forbes and *Zero Stone* by André Norton?

19. The Indian boy Lalu must make a difficult decision. He longs to go away to school and become a doctor. But his ailing father needs Lalu, the oldest son, to help with the farming for his large family. What book is this?

20. In what book does a school bus tip over in a blizzard and burn? A young teacher and seven pupils must find shelter from the storm that blows and howls for eight bitterly cold days and nights. Their only food is the lunches the children carry.

21. Chris, a boy in his teens, deeply resents Calvin Fitch, his stepfather. He wants to keep secret from him the wild German shepherd dog that he has found, but the dog is too sick for Chris to handle without help. What book is this?

22. In what book is a stone cracked into two pieces by error? The Lodge of Masons christen the stone, then carry it on a stretcher, in a mock funeral procession, to the dumping ground.
    Clue: The crowd in the town is so amused that they throw the Masons enough coins to pay for the spoiled stone.

23. When Alison traces the pattern from a delicately bordered dinner plate, a series of strange happenings begin which compel her and two friends, Roger and Gwyn, to take parts in the Welsh valley's violent legend of love and death. What book is this?
    Clue: The border on the plate looks like flowers to most people but like owls to the people of the valley.

24. These people are characters in what Newbery Medal book?

a) A boy who hates the Romans for killing his father.

b) A huge slave who cannot hear or speak.

c) A group of rebels in a cave.

25. In what book do two English boys, one a city evacuee and one whose brother is scorned as a conscientious objector, risk their lives to cross the English Channel to rescue troops from Dunkirk?
Clue: Both boys' fathers are involved in the war.

26. Fifteen-year-old Corey Tremaine is bound to a Mormon family going West, and betrothed to a stepson of the family. But her fiancé goes against Mormon ideas when he helps the sick with medicine, and is finally ordered out of the wagon train. Corey is left to care for his dying mother. What book tells this story?

27. What book tells of a friendly sergeant in the German army, famous as a soccer player, who has been stationed in a French coastal village for several years during World War II? The day before the Allied invasion, a German officer is shot, and the sergeant is ordered to have six hostages killed. Three of the hostages are his friends.

28. A girl whose mother has recently died resents the attention paid to her father by another woman. When the woman brings a huge fresh coconut cake to the house, the girl dumps it into the pig trough. What book is this?

29. Name the book in which a young man is in a tremendous stone prison, accused of defrauding the Spanish king. His jailer eagerly waits for him to finish a map to a vast buried treasure.
Clue: The treasure is leather bags full of gold dust.

30. A young bride, new to living in the wilderness in 1889, receives what she thinks are strange gifts—from her husband a rifle, a fishing rod and rubber boots, and from his sister a pair of long loose pants. She will not wear these unusual, "improper" clothes, or go hunting with her husband, until one day he calls her a foolish prig. Then she goes off alone in the forest to hunt and becomes hopelessly lost. Can you name the book?

31. In what book is a girl called a witch because she is deaf and dumb, she has large searching eyes, and she cared for a baby who died?

32. Can you identify this book from the following clues?
    a) A strange woman gives the principal of a Negro school one hundred dollars for white paint, so the school can "shine like a beacon."
    b) A black boy, David, and a white boy, Little Red, are swept over a dam when David jumps in the water to save Little Red.
    c) A black man is arrested for "disturbing the peace" because he asks for the same wages as a white man.

33. David, a sophomore at college, feels suspended between the Jim Crow role thrust at him by white people, and the "progressive symbol" role thrust at him by his parents. What book is this?

34. Here are three clues to a book. Can you give the title?
    a) A boy named Jethro.
    b) His cousin Eb, a deserter from the Union Army.
    c) A letter from President Lincoln.

35. In what book does a girl in her teens, who had been captured by the Indians, finally get to Montreal where she earns a living for herself, her sister and two nieces by making dresses for wealthy French women?

36. In what book is sixteen-year-old Candace (Dacie) Tybott determined to have more education than was considered proper for a girl at the time of the American Revolution? When the schoolmaster goes off to war, Dacie becomes a teacher. Among her students is Drusilla, a freed slave who had been rescued from a shipwreck by Dacie's father.

37. In what book does the Lord of the Eagles bring about the rescue of a wizard named Gandalf and his fourteen companions from a fierce pack of wolves and an army of goblins?
Clue: In this book a jewel called the Arkenstone is of great importance.

38. In a story of the Dark Ages, what young son of a Viking chief, through his pride and arrogance, pleases the elderly king of Denmark so greatly that the king names him his heir? But when the old king dies his wishes are not carried out.

39. In the Stone Age story *And the Waters Prevailed* by D. Moreau Barringer, how did Andor's tribe react when he warned them of a great flood that would bury their village in a valley that we now call the Mediterranean Sea?

40. Ranofer, a young Egyptian boy who longs to be a goldsmith, is offered, as a reward for bravery, the chance to name the thing he craves most in the

world. He asks for a donkey. Tell why, and name this book.

Clue: After Ranofer's father dies, he is forced to become an apprentice to a stonecutter.

41. What twelve-year-old South Korean boy is captured by the Chinese Communists when they raid his home and set fire to his village? Since he speaks some English, they want to use him as a "Little Devil," to spy on American prisoners.

42. Unlike other high school freshmen, Albert Scully doesn't like sports or rock'n'roll, but enjoys Beethoven, Shakespeare and Thoreau. He is not accepted by his classmates or by himself. Only when his mother sends him to complain to an old lady in the neighborhood about burning garbage does life begin to be better for Albert in the book ___ ___ ___.

43. In what book does a boy named Mel win a music contest and then face the hypocrisy of a hotel manager, Mr. Nash, who wants to add a large check of his own to the prize?

Clue: Mr. Nash had previously refused to have Mel and two friends served in the hotel restaurant.

44. Neighbors and teachers readily believe that Butch Reece is guilty of stealing at school. His father is a drunkard, his home is the worst in the village, and the boy is tough. A few people, among them the school principal and a farmer, believe Butch is innocent. Butch knows who stole, but he won't tell. What book is this?

Clue: The boy who did the stealing has told Butch that his mother is ill and might have a fatal heart attack at any time.

45. What teen-age girl trains her falcon, Zander, to hunt, and then doesn't want to fly him in a meet because she is afraid of losing him?

46. Who was the twelve-year-old London boy who picked a piece of paper out of a wealthy-looking man's pocket, then found he was being hunted by two men in brown? Because he could not read, he did not understand why the men would kill him to get the paper.
    Clue: The book title is the boy's name.

47. Don Harvey is attending a ranch school in New Mexico when an unexpected radiogram comes from his parents, requesting his immediate departure for Mars, where they are working. In the next twenty-four hours Don is questioned by security police in New Chicago, a family friend disappears, and Don finds himself in possession of a cheap but possibly valuable ring which he is to deliver to his father, if he can get to Mars. What book is this?

48. A boy, half buried in the ruins of his defeated town, is found by an elephant whose driver persuades the boy to join the conquering army. The army is led by one of history's famous generals. Can you name this book?

49. In *Hold Fast to Your Dreams* by Catherine Blanton, fifteen-year-old Emmy Lou leaves Blossom, Alabama, and goes to Mesa, Arizona, to pursue her ambition. Despite many disappointments, she holds fast to her dream. What was that dream?

50. It was squat and black and half as tall as a man. Its ugly mouth gaped wide enough to hold a human body. Its rim was crooked and battered, its sides

dented and scarred, and everywhere on it were dark brown flecks which were not rust. What was it?

Clue: It was used for turning dead people into fierce, merciless warriors who could not be killed.

51. In what book do three Australian boys save a country wedding for a weeping bride? The bride's father is behind on his bills and the caterer has refused the job, so the boys help with both the wedding and the reception in exchange for three old horses, saddles and bridles.

Clue: The boys have accepted a challenge to travel nine hundred miles, using no modern transportation and spending no money.

52. In what Newbery Medal book does a boy lose his cat in the basement of a New York apartment building, and another boy pick a lock to help him get the cat?

53. Captain Crane sank his harpoon into the whale, but his leg was caught in the running line and had to be amputated. What book is this?

54. Fifteen-year-old Jørn defies his father and goes to spend his summer vacation with an older friend, Ulf. The vacation begins with a sudden, middle of the night departure on a sailboat that Ulf claims is his. Jørn doesn't explore his suspicions, even when Ulf insists on repainting the boat and altering the rigging. Can you name this book?

55. Tom Curtis is a high school senior with a tough decision to make. He wants more than anything to be a jazz musician, and when an offer comes to

him, he must choose between college or music *now*. Name this book.

56. The many languages he learned in a concentration camp are a help to David when he escapes and heads on foot across Europe, carrying only a compass, a knife, a piece of soap and a bottle of water. What book is this?

57. Roley Rolandson was faced with permanent blindness at the age of nineteen. Feeling sorry for himself, he gave up his ambition of becoming a doctor. What brought him out of his depression and what is the title of the book?

58. What book tells of Jake Hanlon, who rides a mustang in a 530-mile race from Deadwood to Omaha? Ten men and a great deal of money are involved in the race. When Jake and only three others are still riding, trouble comes in the shape of bribes and drugs.

59. What Indian boy, after risking his life to capture a wild white stallion and his herd, cut the horses' hobbles and set them free so that he could ride to warn his village of an enemy attack?

60. Benjamin Brown escapes from cruel labor in an English cotton mill and arrives in New York during the exciting Federalist era. He comes to the attention of Thomas Jefferson, who puts him through college, in the book __ __ __.

61. When Rebecca is conducted to a black chair at the spot where she is to be burned as a sorceress, she calls for a champion. What knight comes forth to defend her?

62. In what book is a boy, Griff Gunston, on an island with a few native inhabitants and a group of navy men when atomic war begins? The island becomes isolated from the rest of the world.
Clue: Near the island is an ugly breed of octopuses capable of waging war on mankind.

63. A falcon is a hawk trained to hunt. Do you know the story in which a boy sets out to search the far North for a rare white hawk in order to ransom his father from the Vikings?

64. In what story by Walter Edmonds does a boy of sixteen help a girl and her partially paralyzed father escape from a group of Indians and British who are burning the settlements along the Mohawk Valley?

65. A young runaway boy finds an unusual dog who looks as if he started out to be a hound and then decided he'd look better as a porcupine. What did he call the dog?
Clue: Big stiff hairs that look exactly like pine needles grow out of the dog's face.

66. In what book is a boy more afraid of performing before a large audience of people than of hunting a bloodthirsty cougar?
Clue: The cougar has killed many sheep.

67. In what book does a 17-year-old high school drop-out-turned-boxer crawl under bushes and into a cave in Central Park to help a friend who has been injured in a grocery store robbery?

68. In what book does a girl wear to her wedding a beautiful black cashmere dress she and her mother had made, an old sage-green bonnet with blue lining, and a gold pin borrowed from her mother, so

that she would be wearing something old and something new, something borrowed and something blue?

69. What boy, alone in total darkness deep in a cave, uses these two natural phenomena to help him find his way out?
    a) The passage of bats on their way out of the cave to feed in the early evening.
    b) The flow of water in a stream.

70. In what book does a lonely boy leave a cattle station in Australia at night and head into the desert with a dog named Rags, because Rags is to be taken away and trained to be leader of a dog pack?

71. A boy has collected the pictures of a great pro halfback, Big Ernie, for years, because he thinks Big Ernie may be his father. The boy lives where?

72. White men moved closer and closer to the last remaining village of the Yahi Indians, so the six Indians found a more hidden place to live—a bear's den—in what book?
    Clue: Later a man from a museum was taken to this Yahi world by one of these Indians.

73. Old King Theseus of Athens kidnaps the youngest princess of Sparta and takes her away in his chariot. The man who stops him is known by what name? The answer is the title of a book by Olivia Coolidge.

74. There is a title hidden in this couplet from an old Negro spiritual. Can you find the title and explain its significance?
    "I thought I heard them say
    There were Lions in the way"

75. In what book does a man lower a baby and a little

girl down into a well? Then the man covers himself with a wet blanket and lies down by the well, because a huge fire is burning toward them. The fire was started accidentally by three young people on a camping trip.

76. In what book does a boy of fourteen run away from a monastery where, as a novice for nineteen months, he has been helping Brother Ernulf, who is surly and disagreeable but a fine artist?
Clue: He runs away after three boys from his family come to visit and make fun of him, as they have done all his life.

77. In what exciting mystery, set on the Isle of Skye, does a boy suspect that his older brother's fall from a bridge into a rocky gorge is not an accident?
Clue: The younger boy takes over his brother's job to try to prove his suspicion.

78. In what book does a boy who has only one useful arm fail his manhood test because he does not kill his wolf? He must leave the village and go to the hills to tend sheep.
Clue: He cannot wear the red wool woven for him by his mother, because only warriors of the tribe can wear that color.

79. In what story of postwar Europe does a silver paper knife help three Polish children find their parents in Switzerland after more than five years of separation?
Clue: The three children and a friend walked from Warsaw, Poland, to Switzerland.

80. Jean Campbell, a high school junior, suffers horribly at her first dance, for she is wearing the wrong dress and her date is rude and indifferent. Soon

after this she goes to an island in Maine to work at a resort. Mary Stolz wrote the book. Can you name it?

81. On a primitive raft, which they made themselves and named in honor of a legendary sun-king of the Incas, the author of this book and five companions voyaged 4,300 miles across the Pacific to Polynesia. What book tells their story?

82. In what book does a twelve-year-old boy, who wants most of all to see a play, struggle to prove himself a good page to his cousin, Sir John, in London?

83. A young prince named Ajor won a victory for his people, but his father was disturbed because Ajor had acted boldly and independently of other princes, not according to custom. Now Ajor says the booty, 252 camels, belongs to the widows of slain men. His father says, "Booty belongs to the Princes . . . That has always been the custom. If they think it is fitting, the Princes will share it with the people. Do you want to alter our customs, my son?" Name this book.

84. A spelunker enters a cave alone, searching for a cave which he could develop into a tourist attraction. He finds the cave but, shaken by an accident, doesn't file his claim. Name this book.

85. In what book does the youngest son of a wealthy tradesman in an ancient city skip school and then buy gold for a bribe to his teacher?

cAnswers

1. *Dead Reckoning* by Victor Mays.

2. *Classmates by Request* by Hila Colman.

3. *Requiem for a Princess* by Ruth M. Arthur.

4. *Mary Emma and Company* by Ralph Moody (this incident also appears at the very end of the book *Man of the Family* by Ralph Moody).

5. *Calico Bush* by Rachel Field.

6. *The Hound of Ulster* by Rosemary Sutcliff.

7. *Up a Road Slowly* by Irene Hunt.

8. *Ladder to the Sky* by Ruth F. Chandler.

9. *Fire Hunter.*

10. Sterling, in the book *Rascal* by Sterling North.

11. *The Young Unicorns* by Madeleine L'Engle.

12. The land is Narnia, and the books are *The Lion, the Witch and the Wardrobe*, *Prince Caspian*, or five others by C. S. Lewis.

13. *Deirdre* by Madeleine Polland.

14. Henry Reed, in the book *Henry Reed's Baby-Sitting Service* by Keith Robertson.

15. *Kavik, the Wolf Dog* by Walt Morey.

16. *The Little Fishes* by Erik Christian Haugaard.

17. *Ring the Judas Bell* by James Forman.

18. In both books the leading character is an apprentice: Johnny Tremain to a silversmith and Murdoc Jern to a gemologist.

IV: ANSWERS / 111

19. *The White Bungalow* by Aimée Sommerfelt.

20. *Winter Thunder* by Mari Sandoz.

21. *Smoke* by William Corbin.

22. *The Book of Hugh Flower* by Lorna Beers.

23. *The Owl Service* by Alan Garner.

24. *The Bronze Bow* by Elizabeth George Speare.

25. *The Dolphin Crossing* by Jill Paton Walsh.

26. *Wilderness Bride* by Annabel and Edgar Johnson.

27. *His Enemy, His Friend* by John R. Tunis.

28. *The Rock and the Willow* by Mildred Lee.

29. *The King's Fifth* by Scott O'Dell.

30. *Love Is Forever* by Margaret E. Bell.

31. *A Single Light* by Maia Wojciechowska.

32. *South Town* by Lorenz Graham.

33. *Who Wants Music on Monday?* by Mary Stolz.

34. *Across Five Aprils* by Irene Hunt.

35. *Calico Captive* by Elizabeth George Speare.

36. *Petticoat Rebel* by Mary Stetson Clarke.

37. *The Hobbit* by J. R. R. Tolkien.

38. *Beorn the Proud* by Madeleine Polland.

39. They scoffed at him and refused to move.

40. In *The Golden Goblet* by Eloise Jarvis McGraw, Ranofer wants a donkey to carry papyrus stalks, so he can sell them and earn enough money to become a pupil of a great goldsmith.

41. Pong Choolie, in the book *Pong Choolie, You Rascal!* by Lucy Herndon Crockett.

42. *The Dream Watcher* by Barbara Wersba.

43. *A Question of Harmony* by Gretchen Sprague.

44. *The Pit* by Reginald Maddock.

45. June Pritchard, in *The Summer of the Falcon* by Jean George.

46. *Smith* by Leon Garfield.

47. *Between Planets* by Robert A. Heinlein.

48. *I Marched with Hannibal* by Hans Baumann.

49. Emmy Lou wants to be a dancer.

50. The black cauldron, in the book of that name by Lloyd Alexander.

51. *Euloowirree Walkabout* by John Kiddell.

52. *It's Like This, Cat* by Emily Cheney Neville.

53. *I, Adam* by Jean Fritz.

54. *Undertow* by Finn Havrevold.

55. *Jazz Country* by Nat Hentoff.

56. *North to Freedom* by Anne S. Holm.

57. Mick, his guide dog, in the book *Guide Dog* by Dorothy Clewes.

58. *Mavericks* by Jack Schaefer.

59. Young Elk, in *The Horsecatcher* by Mari Sandoz.

60. *The Glorious Conspiracy* by Joanne S. Williamson.

61. Ivanhoe, in the book of that name by Sir Walter Scott.

62. *Sea Siege* by André Norton.

63. *Ice Falcon* by Rita Ritchie.

64. *Wilderness Clearing* by Walter D. Edmonds.

65. Bristle Face, in the book of that name by Zachary Ball.

66. *The Ordeal of the Young Hunter* by Jonreed Lauritzen.

67. *The Contender* by Robert Lipsyte.

68. *These Happy Golden Years* by Laura Ingalls Wilder.

69. Peter, in *All the Dark Places* by J. Allan Bosworth.

70. *Boy Alone* by Reginald Ottley.

71. On Durango Street, in the book *Durango Street* by Frank Bonham.

72. *Ishi, Last of His Tribe* by Theodora Kroeber.

73. Agamemnon, known as "The King of Men," in the book *The King of Men.*

74. *Lions in the Way* by Bella Rodman. It is the story of the partial desegregation of a Southern high school, and the "lions" are the agitators who try to stop the integration.

75. *Ash Road* by Ivan Southall.

76. *One Is One* by Barbara Leonie Picard.

77. *Master of Morgana* by Allan Campbell McLean.

78. *Warrior Scarlet* by Rosemary Sutcliff.

79. *The Silver Sword* by Ian Serraillier.

80. *The Sea Gulls Woke Me.*

81. *Kon-Tiki* by Thor Heyerdahl.

82. *I Will Adventure* by Elizabeth Janet Gray.

83. *Adventure in the Desert* by Herbert Kaufmann.

84. *Cave of Danger* by Bryce Walton.

85. *The Three Brothers of Ur* by Jennifer G. Fyson.

Index

In the entries following, Roman numerals identify sections of the book, while Arabic numerals identify questions within the sections. For example, IV–34 refers to question 34 in Section IV (For Older Readers). Running heads in the text carry section numbers to facilitate finding the reference.

Ark, The (Margot Benary-Isbert), III–20
Arthur, Ruth M., IV–3
Artzybasheff, Boris, II–25
Asbjörnsen, Peter C., I–3; II–55
Ash Road (Ivan Southall), IV–75
Ask Mr. Bear! (Marjorie Flack), I–35
Atwater, Florence and Richard, III–152
Away Goes Sally (Elizabeth Coatsworth), II–74

Bailey, Carolyn Sherwin, II–46
Baker, Augusta, III–9
Baker, Betty, III–142
Ball, Zachary, IV–65
Banner in the Sky (James Ramsey Ullman), III–161
Barrie, James M., III–144
Barringer, D. Moreau, IV–39
Battle of St. George Without, The (Janet McNeill), III–151
Baudouy, Michel-Aimé, III–129
Baum, L. Frank, III–145
Baumann, Hans, IV–48
Bawden, Nina, III–65
Bear Called Paddington, A (Michael Bond), II–13
Bear Party (William Pène du Bois), I–37
Bears on Hemlock Mountain, The (Alice Dalgliesh), II–11
Becker, John, II–67
Bedtime for Frances (Russell Hoban), I–24
Bee-Man of Orn, The (Frank R. Stockton), II–43
Beers, Lorna, IV–22
Behn, Harry, II–57
Beim, Jerrold and Lorraine, II–31
Bell, Margaret E., III–133; IV–30

Belling the Tiger (Mary Stolz), I–77
Belting, Natalia M., III–61
Bemelmans, Ludwig, I–74
Ben and Me (Robert Lawson), III–5
Benary-Isbert, Margot, III–20
Benjie (Joan M. Lexau), I–9
Bennett, Anna Elizabeth, II–52
Beorn the Proud (Madeleine Polland), IV–38
Berna, Paul, III–35
Betsy's Little Star (Carolyn Haywood), II–61
Between Planets (Robert A. Heinlein), IV–47
Big Blue Island (Wilson Gage), III–26
Biggest Bear, The (Lynd Ward), II–23
Big Snow, The (Berta and Elmer Hader), I–21
Big Susan (Elizabeth Orton Jones), II–37
Big Wave, The (Pearl S. Buck), III–68
Billy and Blaze (C. W. Anderson), II–86
Birkin (Joan Phipson), III–30
Bishop, Claire Huchet, II–66; III–110
Black Beauty (Anna Sewell), III–139
Black Cauldron, The (Lloyd Alexander), IV–50
Blanton, Catherine, IV–49
Blueberries for Sal (Robert McCloskey), I–63
Bond, Michael, II–13
Bonham, Frank, IV–71
Bontemps, Arna, II–19
Bonzon, Paul-Jacques, III–41
Book of Hugh Flower, The (Lorna Beers), IV–22
Book of Nursery and Mother Goose Rhymes (compiled and illustrated by Marguerite

Mehdevi, Anne Sinclair, III–53
Melindy's Medal (George Faulkner and John Becker), II–67
Merrill, Jean, III–54
Middle Moffat, The (Eleanor Estes), III–55
Mike Mulligan and His Steam Shovel (Virginia Lee Burton), I–16, 71
Mike's House (Julia L. Sauer), I–16
Miles, Miska, I–81
Milhous, Katherine, I–60
Millions of Cats (Wanda Gág), I–32
Milne, A. A., I–55; III–51
Minarik, Else Holmelund, I–87; II–2
Mine for Keeps (Jean Little), III–95
Minnow Leads to Treasure, The (Philippa Pearce), III–176
Miss Bianca (Margery Sharp), III–163
Miss Happiness and Miss Flower (Rumer Godden), III–28
Miss Hickory (Carolyn Sherwin Bailey), II–46
Miss Pickerell Goes to Mars (Ellen MacGregor), III–49
Missing Melinda (Jacqueline Jackson), II–53
Mr. De Luca's Horse (Marjorie Paradis), III–81
Mr. Popper's Penguins (Florence and Richard Atwater), III–152
Mister Stormalong (Ann Malcolmson and Dell J. McCormick), III–23
Mitten, The (Alvin Tresselt), I–17
Mittens (Clare Turlay Newberry), I–45
Mizumura, Kazue, I–76
Moe, Jörgen I., I–3; II–55
Molarsky, Osmond, II–22

Mommy, Buy Me a China Doll (Harvé and Margot Zemach), I–33
Montgomery, Rutherford, III–17
Moody, Ralph, III–171; IV–4
Moominpappa at Sea (Tove Jansson), III–168
Moon Jumpers, The (Janice May Udry), I–40
Moon Tenders, The (August Derleth), III–147
More All-of-a-Kind Family (Sydney Taylor), III–89
Morey, Walt, III–79; IV–15
Mosel, Arlene, I–78
Mother Goose, I–1, 12, 36, 92
Mother Goose: Seventy-seven Verses (pictures by Tasha Tudor), I–36
Mouse and His Child, The (Russell Hoban), III–175
Mousewife, The (Rumer Godden), I–65
Muku, Hatoju, II–69
My Brother Stevie (Eleanor Clymer), III–97
My Dog Rinty (Ellen Tarry and Marie Hall Ets), II–1
My Father's Dragon (Ruth S. Gannett), II–49
My Friend Mac (May McNeer and Lynd Ward), II–39
My Mother Is the Most Beautiful Woman in the World (Rebecca H. Reyher), II–71
My Side of the Mountain (Jean George), III–109

Namesake: A Story of King Alfred, The (C. Walter Hodges), III–98
Ness, Evaline, I–53; II–17
Neville, Emily Cheney, III–59; IV–52
Newberry, Clare Turlay, I–45

Nic Leodhas, Sorche, I–52; III–
150
Nightbirds on Nantucket (Joan
Aiken), III–159
North, Sterling, IV–10
North to Freedom (Anne S.
Holm), IV–56
North Wind and the Sun, The
(Jean de la Fontaine, illus-
trated by Brian Wildsmith),
I–13
Norton, André, IV–18, 62
Norton, Mary, III–19, 121
*Nothing Ever Happens on My
Block* (Ellen Raskin), I–54

O'Dell, Scott, III–90; IV–29
Old One-Toe (Michel-Aimé
Baudoy), III–129
"Old Woman and Her Pig, The"
(Joseph Jacobs), I–23
Old Woman and Her Pig, The
(retold and illustrated by Paul
Galdone), I–23
On the Banks of Plum Creek
(Laura Ingalls Wilder), III–
148
One Is One (Barbara Leonie
Picard), IV–76
One Monday Morning (Uri
Shulevitz), I–30
Onion John (Joseph Krumgold),
III–111
*Ordeal of the Young Hunter,
The* (Jonreed Lauritzen), IV–
66
Ormondroyd, Edward, I–41
Orphans of Simitra, The (Paul-
Jacques Bonzon), III–41
Other Side of the Fence, The
(Molly Cone), II–70
Ottley, Reginald, III–140; IV–70
Otto in Africa (William Pène
du Bois), I–86
Owl Service, The (Alan
Garner), IV–23

Pancakes-Paris (Claire Huchet
Bishop), II–66
Paradis, Marjorie, III–81
Parkinson, Ethelyn M., III–16
Parrish, Anne, II–20
Pearce, Philippa, III–80, 176
*Pecos Bill: The Greatest Cowboy
of All Time* (James Bow-
man), III–4
Perilous Road, The (William
Owen Steele), III–22
Persian Folk and Fairy Tales
(Anne Sinclair Mehdevi),
III–53
Peterkin Papers, The (Lucretia
P. Hale), III–77
Peter Pan (James M. Barrie),
III–144
Petersham, Maud and Miska,
I–2
Peter's Moose (Hughie Call)
II–64
Petticoat Rebel (Mary Stetson
Clarke), IV–36
Petunia, I Love You (Roger
Duvoisin), II–14
Peyton, K. M., III–160
Phipson, Joan, III–30, 122
Picard, Barbara Leonie, IV–76
Pinky Pye (Eleanor Estes), III–
125
Piper, Watty, I–93
Pippi Longstocking (Astrid
Lindgren), III–103
Pit, The (Reginald Maddock),
IV–44
Pitschi (Hans Fischer), I–39
Pocketful of Cricket, A
(Rebecca Caudill), I–80
Politi, Leo, I–75
Polland, Madeleine, III–153;
IV–13, 38
Pong Choolie, You Rascal!
(Lucy Herndon Crockett),
IV–41
Poppy in the Corn, A (Stella
Weaver), III–75